# HOW TO MAKE A KILLING
# IN THE SHARE JUNGLE

# HOW TO MAKE A KILLING IN THE SHARE JUNGLE

MICHAEL WALTERS

SIDGWICK & JACKSON
LONDON

*First published in Great Britain in 1986 by*
*Sidgwick & Jackson Limited*

*Copyright © 1986 by Michael Walters*

*ISBN 0–283–99376–6*

*Phototypeset by Falcon Graphic Art Ltd*
*Wallington, Surrey*

*Printed in Great Britain by Anchor Brendon Ltd*
*Colchester, Essex*
*for Sidgwick & Jackson Limited*
*1 Tavistock Chambers, Bloomsbury Way*
*London WC1A 2SG*

# Contents

*To Maggie, who has a share in everything*

# Introduction

Safer than the 3.30 at Chepstow, more fun than the football pools, better than breaking the bank at Monte Carlo – a fortunate few make millions playing the stock market every year, some by luck, some by judgement. Anyone can play. You may not make the millionaire club, but even the most modest investors can multiply their money many times over. You, too, can make a killing in the share jungle.

The City is changing. The 'Big Bang' of October 1986, has shaken the system to the core. And with a Conservative government eager to encourage the individual investor and backing share sales of such organizations as British Gas, the Trustees Savings Bank, British Airports Authority and more, the mood is dramatically different. And from January 1987, the tax advantages of the new Personal Equity Plans (PEP) make individual share ownership a real plus.

Suddenly, share dealing is coming alive for the small investor. The notion that the big institutions – insurance companies and pension funds – would proceed to total domination of the share market is being pushed back. The British Telecom bonanza began the challenge, attracting 2 million investors, half of them buying shares for the first time. Very nicely they did, too. Most stayed on, resisting the temptation to cash in when they could have more than doubled their money within months.

In the spring of 1986, even the Stock Exchange was shocked – and delighted – to discover in a Treasury survey that there were more than 6 million shareholders in Britain – twice as many as had been assumed, and double the number in 1979. The survey also showed you do not have to be rich to join the shareholding democracy. One shareholder in five had income of less than £9500 a year, and more than one in three earned less than £13,500.

And small shareholders have been doing well. Since January 1975 when the Financial Times Index – the main measure of share values – slumped to 146, the market has been roaring ahead: in April 1986, the FT Index topped 1425 – nearly ten times higher.

Many shares rose much more than ten-fold. In 1974, shares in Grand Metropolitan, the brewing, dairy and leisure giant, were 24p; by the spring of 1986, they were 430p. And BOC, the former British Oxygen Company, rocketed from 14½p to 345p. Others did even better. First National Finance almost went bust in 1975, when its shares sold at less than 1p each; by May 1986, however they were 210p. If you had invested £5000 in them in 1975, you would have been a millionaire in 1986. Not bad.

That is not all. There are few who have not heard the tale of Polly Peck, the ailing rag trade company which came to life when Turkish-Cypriot economics graduate Asil Nadir bought in and transformed it into a fruit-trading and electronics empire based in his native land. In three years, the shares soared from 9p to touch £36. That time around, it took a mere £2500 to become a millionaire – in three years.

Polly Peck faded, of course, and the shares fell back. Three years after the peak, they had halved. If the £2500 millionaires had stayed aboard, they would be down to their last £500,000. Not too bad.

Share trading can be a gamble, but the odds are not impossible. They are much better than the gee-gees, the pools or the casino. Get it wrong with them and you have lost all of your stake money. On the stock market, however, few companies go bust, few investors lose everything, and although a reckless gambler can be wiped out quickly, it takes some doing. Shares rise and fall in relatively gentle bursts. There is usually time enough to change your mind, to sell without too much damage if you have made a mistake, or see something you fancy more.

And now the barriers are coming crashing down. The snooty City, the City that turned away the man and woman in the street, is opening up and welcoming them in. The Big Bang means 200 years of trading history are being overturned. Hundreds of millions of pounds are being invested to keep pace with the global explosion in share trading. And much of it will make life easier for the small investor.

Suddenly, the City wants small investors and their money. Not every firm has thrown the doors wide open yet, but there is a real revolution. Stockbrokers galore are gearing themselves up to trade for the smaller share buyer, offering a variety of services designed to cut dealing costs, and to make the system simple and accessible to all. They are promoting their wares in the press. Some even appear on TV. Share shops are opening in the High Street, inviting you to buy and sell on the spot. Major store chains are examining ways they can offer financial advice. Banks, and even building societies, are thinking how they can help in the share-buying boom.

The new Personal Equity Plan, unveiled in the 1986 Budget, allows everyone to invest up to £2400 a year in shares tax-free. Provided this is kept in shares for at least a calendar year (the whole of 1987, or the whole of 1988, etc.), any capital growth or income on the cash will be entirely free of tax. It is a fairly modest beginning, but the start of an exciting new political initiative to boost the numbers of small investors. And the City loves it. A whole host of schemes is being launched to catch new clients, with unit trusts, investment trusts, brokers and others holding out welcoming arms.

For the first time, the City and the stock market are going out to sell themselves to the public. For the first time, stockbrokers can sell shares which they themselves own. They may even telephone you at home with news of something for you to buy.

It means exciting new opportunities – and new dangers. The prospective share buyer is going to be wooed as never before, but will need to take care. The City is still a dangerous place for the unwary. There will be good, honest, well-meaning advice galore – and there will be pressure to sell, sell, sell. Some will cut corners. The share-dealing jungle will claim a few victims.

This book offers a practical, sympathetic guide through that jungle. I have been there. For 25 years, I have been watching and writing about the wheelers and the dealers, the winners and the losers, tipping shares which have soared, and the odd one which has slumped.

There is a lot to learn, and I have learned some of it the hard way, buying and selling shares myself. The theory matters, and there are worthy works explaining it. But until you get on the inside, doing it yourself, there is something missing. Practice can be very different from the theory.

I know how it feels – the thump in the pit of the stomach, the dizzy whirl around the brain – to get caught with a share which goes wrong. And the sheer elation of spotting a winner, watching it rocket. Everyday share dealing does not always work the way you expect. There are tricks and treats, short-cuts and sly precautions. Some of them are in this book. I hope they help.

Do not be put off by what might appear to be a mass of technical detail. It helps to know about it, but you can get by without it, if you wish. There are money-making opportunities galore – in the new-issue boom, bid stocks, asset situations, shell companies, under-valued growth stocks, loan stocks and options. They are all there, waiting for you to try.

You do not need a fortune. You do not need to understand all of the jargon, to have masses of research at your finger tips. Some of the mightiest investors in the land, sophisticated beyond belief, scanned an offer to back computer boffin Sir Clive Sinclair in 1984. They clamoured for shares at £34 each. Individual investors were locked out. This was a bonanza for the big boys. Two years later, Sinclair Research was struggling. Sir Clive sold off most of what was left, and the shares slumped to 60p.

Even the experts get it wrong. You may be smarter – or luckier. In the end, all you need is common sense, and luck. Go to it. Share trading might make you a fortune – it might not. But it certainly can be fun.

# 1 Should You Be in the Stock Market?

*Accentuate the positive, eliminate the negative.* That is not a bad guide to making a killing in the share jungle. There are fortunes to be made in the stock market. Anyone can do it with luck, a little judgement, and perhaps a tip or two to take them through the trickier bits.

This book is dedicated to the positive thinkers who want to go out and do it. However, it would be foolish to suggest that everyone can be a winner, irresponsible to say that everyone ought to hammer ahead and try it. Take care. It is dangerous out there.

Certain people should never be allowed near the stock market, but there are no rules, no laws to stop them. Trying to prevent a fool and his money being parted can be a fruitless task. Just make sure that you are not among the fools.

Before you start planning that penthouse in town, the villa in Spain and the other trimmings that come with making a fortune in the stock market, pause a moment. And pause again. Share dealing can be a risky business. No matter how careful you are, you can lose money at it – all of your money. Companies do not go bust very often, but some do. If you have your savings in one of them, then you can kiss your cash goodbye. And if you have invested foolishly on borrowed money (oh they do, they do), and the stock market starts to slide, you could end up deeply in debt.

## A SAVAGE PLACE

You could, indeed, have bought shares in Grand Metropolitan, the dairy, brewing and leisure giant, for 24p in 1974, and sold them for over 400p in 1986. Wonderful. But what if you had bought them for 85p earlier in 1974? You would have suffered a swift, savage loss. The bargains a fortunate few picked up in 1974 and 1975 had a very sour taste for those who had bought them two years earlier, and were crippled as they collapsed to bargain basement prices. Who would

1

have thought that in 1975 the stock market would slump to 146? Who would have thought that, in the 1960s, Rolls-Royce could ever go into liquidation? But it did.

What about Jim Slater? An accountant who started tinkering in the stock market, he bought control of a £1.5 million company in 1964, and built it into one of the 50 largest companies in the UK, valued at over £200 million. Much of the growth was generated by Jim's legendary share-dealing ability. Then the ace paper shuffler hit trouble, Slater Walker shares began to slide, and from a peak of 360p, they touched 12p in the secondary banking crisis in the second half of the 1970s. Super share dealer Slater found himself out on his ear, a minus millionaire. He began the long road back writing books for children. Now Jim Slater is comfortably in the millionaire class again, largely on the strength of his share-dealing acumen. Spectacular? Yes. Safe? Forget it.

The stock market can be a savage place. The crash of 1974–75 wrecked marriages, ruined careers and shortened many lives. Legend has them diving out of windows on Wall Street in the great crash of 1929. Hundreds of thousands of Americans had their lives blighted by it, and once-wealthy families were in despair through the Depression of the 1930s. So be warned. Investing in the stock market can seem warm and cosy when you are winning, but it can turn cold, hard and terribly costly, without warning. Never forget, it is a risky business, and the risks may be too great for you.

## CUTTING THE RISKS

That said, it is simple to cut those risks down to size. Before you take the plunge, go through the boring basics. Everyone ought to do it. They are plain, simple and totally fundamental. Stripped down, they mean that you can only afford to play if you can afford to lose every penny you put up. So think very carefully about what you can afford to spend.

If you are married, you should own your home and be comfortably able to cover the mortgage payments each month. If you are not married, or prefer to rent a place to live in, be sure you can cover the cost of accommodation. Check you are properly insured. For the married man or woman, that means life insurance – perhaps for ten times your annual salary. If you are the breadwinner, you should also have permanent health insurance, so that there is a guaranteed income if you are unable to continue working. You should also have some savings in the National Savings Investment Bank or in a building society – somewhere dull, boring and safe.

2

# HOW MUCH YOU NEED TO PLAY THE MARKET

Only after all safety systems are in place should anyone begin seriously to think about buying shares. Although you can spend as little as £25 (say £10 for a share or two and £15 for the cost of getting someone to buy them for you), you really need at least £500, preferably more. If you are even half serious about wanting to make money at it, you need at least £1000. That will allow you to split your cash between shares in two companies and to make a reasonable return, after expenses, if you get it right.

## UNIT TRUSTS

If you have set up all your safeguards and have enough money to spend, as a first step perhaps you should consider a unit trust. Unit trusts invest in shares, and split the rights to those shares between everyone who has bought a piece of that trust – a unit. The units rise or fall according to the value of the shares the trust holds. Most trusts have between 40 and 120 shares, so buying into a unit trust gives you a little piece of the action in 40 to 120 shares. The trust manager should be clued up about investment, and should pick winners on your behalf, taking the troublesome part of investment off your hands.

That is the theory, and it works fairly well. The trouble is that there are unit trust companies galore, each offering a range of trusts (there are around 1000 of them) trying to do different things. Some buy shares in the United States, Australia, Europe or the Far East. Others go for leisure or technology companies. Others concentrate on the best capital growth or the highest return. Instead of making life simple for the would-be investor, removing the puzzle over which shares to buy, they have substituted a new puzzle – which unit trust to buy?

In spite of this, the average unit trust should be safer for the beginner than going straight into the stock market. Best of all are the growth or income funds operated by big groups who have been around for years. Firms such as M & G or Save & Prosper may not always top the charts, but they do produce good, solid performance. Among the smaller groups, Martyn Arbib has won an enviable reputation for his Perpetual trusts.

3

## THE FUN OF SHARES

There is nothing, though, to say that you have to be at all serious about shares. A large part of the attraction – for the big winners as well as the minnows – is the sheer fun of shares. Scratch any giant industrialist, and you will find he sees much of his money as simply a means of keeping score. The first £500,000 or so is really quite important for what it will buy. After that, the familiar line comes in – you can only eat so many dinners a day, only drive one car at a time, only live in so many houses . . .

The cash becomes squiggles on a bank statement, or the back of an envelope. Does it really matter to Dick Giordano, boss of British Oxygen, whether he earns £800,000 or £900,000 a year? The tax man takes a great slug of it. Maybe he and the other top-ten earners – chaps like Lonrho's Tiny Rowland, Sir Patrick Sergeant at Associated Newspapers, Sir Ralph Halpern at Burton and Gerald Ronson at Heron – would be reluctant to own up in public, but it probably gives them more satisfaction to be seen among the nation's top wage-earners than it does to take home an extra £5000 or even £50,000 a year. As status symbols go, cash goes a long, long way. And if you are not an Olympic athlete, it is a pretty satisfying way of telling the world that you are still a winner.

The same psychology applies to the individual investor. The money is nice, but being right is almost nicer. That warm glow when you spot a share winner and see it soar is really special, like playing Monopoly with real money. You can get the same glow whether you have £50, £500 or £5000 in play. So do not be put off by the notion that you ought to have at least £500 worth of shares in each company you invest in. That is the money man talking. If you want to play for peanuts and enjoy the game simply as a game, go ahead – and good luck. That way, at least, you avoid the sickening feeling that slams into the pit of your stomach when your biggest investment goes wrong. It happens, and believe me, it hurts.

## BE HONEST ABOUT INVESTMENT

Above all, try to be honest about what you want to be in the stock market – and about whether you can cope, not just financially, but emotionally. It is easy to overlook individual feelings. Investing can be a drug, an obsession. I have seen a financial journalist lose first a big house, then a flat and end up in rented rooms, all because of an uncontrollable urge to play the stock market – even though he kept getting it wrong. Do not let the bug get you. Decide how much you can afford to play with, and stick to it. If you lose it, let it go. If you can't, the stock market is not for you.

## HARE OR TORTOISE?

Decide, too, whether you are a hare or a tortoise. Do you want to gamble on shares that will double or go bust quickly? Or are you content to sit and watch, investing in a solid share which will let you sleep at nights while it rises steadily in value?

There is no particular merit in one approach or the other, though a lot of people see greater virtue in the plodder. The greatest investment cop-out is to concentrate on long-term performance. John Maynard Keynes, the great economist, remarked that, in the long term, we are all dead. It is hard to suppress the feeling that if you have not invested in a share which is moving up today, you are missing out. There is time enough to switch to the slower mover tomorrow, when you can afford to play more of a waiting game.

For the beginner, however, choosing a steady share allows more time to learn about what is really going on. No one is going to learn much by buying a share which doubles or halves in a fortnight. That will be put down to beginner's luck, good or bad. Months of watching share prices will give you a feel about an individual share, and about how it behaves in different market moods. That can pay off in helping to select other shares.

Clearly the amount of time and effort you can put into watching investments should also help determine the way you invest. Ideally, the cautious investor will want to study the market long and hard, perhaps selecting a make-believe list of investments, watching for months how they move on paper before actually buying anything. Careful investors spread their risks, splitting cash between several different companies' shares, so that one loser does not drag down the value of the whole portfolio too far.

## CAPITAL GROWTH OR INCOME?

You need to decide too, whether you are in the market for capital growth – an increase in the value of the money you invest – or for income – the amount that the money you invest will earn for you each year as interest or dividends. The two are not mutually exclusive. This book is biased towards the capital-growth seeker, which is where

5

the real stock market fun is. If you want income, insurance-linked products may be best, or perhaps government securities, which we deal with later. If you want some capital growth, and income growth that will outstrip a building society's interest after a few years, go back to a high-income unit trust.

## GOING FOR A GAMBLE

Others will hope to spot special situations, and plunge the lot on them. Spreading the cash may be safer, but it dilutes the impact of any big winners. Finding a fast mover is difficult enough, and when you are convinced you have one, you may want to plunge on it, all or nothing. That strategy will find little support from standard City investment advisers. They will opt every time for the slow, steady route – that way they are protected from accusations of irresponsibility. In appearing to guard your back, they are also guarding their own – one of the first principles of City conduct. It is your money – you make your own rules. But think about it first.

In practice, many first-time investors are looking for an out-and-out gamble. The last thing they want is some boring name from the glorious past of British industry, paying a predictable dividend that barely keeps pace with inflation. They want to treat the Stock Exchange as a kind of glorified casino. And why not? Put all of your cash on the red if you want. Just understand what you are doing. If it all goes wrong, you have no one to blame but yourself.

If you win, hallelujah! Just do not get carried away by it. Never believe that you have found the winning formula: that is a recipe for disaster. One winner and you will be entering the most testing time of your new-found career. You will know just enough to think you can do it – but not enough to understand that you will never know quite enough. Someone, somewhere, always knows more.

## EVERYONE HAS AN ANGLE

Cynical? Perhaps.But cynicism is an essential tool for the would-be investor. There is very little certain about investment – but you can be absolutely certain that everyone has an angle. That angle might mean nothing but good for you, with everyone pulling together to get the same share price higher. Often, the angle will be too well concealed for you to detect, but it will be there. Always ask yourself: what's in it for you – and for the other fellow? That is a crucial investment rule.

6

# 2    Absolute Beginners: Where to Start

You need to know very little to invest on the stock market: the name of a share to buy, the name of a bank or stockbroker to buy it for you, and how to write the cheque to pay for it.

The virgin investor can score by luck alone. One newspaper proved it: opening the back pages of the *Financial Times*, they selected shares by throwing darts at the share listings. This 'Bull's-eye portfolio' beat one picked by City worthies, supposedly skilled in the art of share selection.

You need to know just as much about the City and share investment as you feel you want to. You are never likely to master it all. That way leads to madness and to ruin. If you want to play your hunches, back the tips you get at your local or follow your favourite newspaper share tipster blind, you can.

It is more comfortable, though, to feel you know a little about what you are doing – and more fun. The more you put into it, the more you are likely to get out of it. Who knows – perhaps a working knowledge of the stock market will help swing the investment odds a little your way?

## DO NOT BE INTIMIDATED

Most important of all, try to be realistic about what you know, and what you do not. It is easy to be intimidated by the City, where the air of mystery and tradition, money and power, spiced with a dash of the old school tie and the gentleman's club, can appear distinctly off-putting. The atmosphere has persisted even in the face of tougher competition, the rise of the meritocracy and the new computer-literate number-crunchers. The occasional top hat still surfaces; there are still one or two magnificently sombre wood-panelled offices where the family partners in the merchant bank used to sit. A chap in a pink frock-coat still guards the doors of the Bank of England.

7

All splendid tradition, and long may it linger, but it all serves quietly to emphasize the gentle division between them and us. They, it seems, are steeped in generations of money matters, gifted with a subtle understanding of such things. The rest of us are not quite the same.

Do not fall for it. There are brilliant minds in the City, and there may be fewer fifth generation fools than 20 years ago, but some do cling on. Alongside them are hundreds of thousands of ordinary people doing ordinary jobs, all of them as liable as you are to get a little muddled now and then, and sometimes just as uncertain about things.

## NEVER BE BLINDED BY FIGURES OR JARGON

There is an additional barrier because the City lives by figures. Figures frighten people. It may seem that City folk understand them intimately. Do not be fooled. Some do, some do not.

What matters to you is whether City people make sense to you. They may be leading you up the garden path, they may be lost themselves or they may be showing you the way to investment heaven, but unless you can understand them, forget it. Never hesitate to ask them to slow down, go back and start again. The instant they lose you, stop them – and make them start all over again.

Never, never, let anyone blind you with figures. Never, never, be afraid to appear an absolute idiot. If you do not understand, keep asking until it makes sense. If you cannot get to grips with it, you have found your answer. It is not for you.

Trust yourself. You will be the loser if you get it wrong, if you allow yourself to be blinded by jargon that you did not like to question because you might have sounded foolish. You will feel much more of a fool – a poor fool – if the whole thing goes wrong later. And the part you did not understand is at the root of the problem.

The City and the stock market should be a simple matter of common sense. Stick to what you understand. Ask the questions which seem sensible for you to ask – and make sure you get the answers you want.

## THE LANGUAGE OF THE STOCK MARKET

It does help, however, to be able to follow the basic vocabulary of investment. If some of it seems off-putting, do not worry; you will grow used to it. If some of the arithmetic is a problem, never mind.

You never need to do the sums yourself. The answers are available all over the place – in newspapers, in investment magazines, and on the electronic information services your stockbroker or banker can tap into easily.

If calculating a price-earnings ratio sounds tricky, ask somebody to do it for you. What matters about price-earnings ratios is what they tell you about a particular share, not whether you can work them out. The same applies to the other things.

## What is a share?

What is a share? Easy. Exactly what it says. A share is a part of a business. Say four people get together, and each of them puts £25 into a business. That business will have £100 invested. Each of the four will have one quarter of it, or perhaps 25 shares of £1 each. And so it goes. All quoted companies work roughly the same way: they have millions of shares, each one entitling the holder to an equal part of the company. The more shares you have, the bigger your stake in the company.

People frequently use the words 'stocks' and 'shares' interchangeably. Strictly speaking, however, stocks are securities which earn a fixed rate of interest, whereas dividends on shares rise and fall. And, strictly speaking, some shares are actually called stock units. Technically, for example, ICI does not have shares, but £1 stock units – though there is no practical difference between them and £1 shares in other companies. Do not let the distinction bother you.

## Nominal value

Before the British Gas share issue, British Telecom was our biggest public company. It has shares with a *nominal value* of 25p each. Nominal, or par, value does not matter much. It is simply the face value a company chooses to put on the shares – an accounting convention. In UK companies, it is usually between 1p and £1. All UK shares must, by law, have a nominal value, though American companies often have shares with no par value.

A company can just as easily issue capital of £100,000 in 100,000 shares with a £1 par value as it can 10,000,000 shares of 1p par value. The par or nominal value means nothing in itself. A share with a 1p nominal value is not necessarily worth 1p, nor may a £1 nominal value share be worth £1. Shares are worth what someone will pay for them – the market price – and nothing else. Do not be put off good shares because they have a par value of say 5p and sell in the market at 120p. Conversely, do not think you have a bargain by paying 5p for a share with a nominal value of £1. In practice, the main significance of par or nominal value is in calculating what dividend you actually get.

### Dividends

Dividends are usually described as so many pence per share, or expressed as a percentage of the nominal value of the shares. A 10 per cent dividend means you are paid 10p a share on shares with a nominal value of £1. Shares with a nominal value of 10p pay only 1p a share if a 10 per cent dividend is declared. Most shares are called *Ordinary shares* (or equities), and produce dividends that are decided by the board. These normally rise or fall as profits rise or fall. Dividends are normally paid twice a year, usually as an *interim dividend* (the smaller payment) and as a *final dividend* (a larger amount after the profits for the year are known).

### Fixed-interest capital

Companies have other forms of share capital, but these are paid a fixed rate of dividend or interest. If the company goes bust, investors will be repaid the nominal value of these shares before those holding Ordinary shares. Most fixed-interest capital can be ignored, unless you are seeking a higher income, though we deal with special fixed-interest capital-gains opportunities later. The most widely traded forms of fixed-interest capital are preference stocks, loan stocks and convertible loan stocks.

### Contract notes and share certificates

You are the legal owner of your shares as soon as your broker or banker says he or she has bought them. The City's motto is 'MY WORD IS MY BOND', and the system honours it. The contract note that is sent to you at once confirms the price you paid and the commission charges. It is legal proof of ownership, so keep it safe. It will be needed when you complete your tax return. A few weeks later, you will be sent a share certificate from the company's registrars, who keep details of all shareholdings. Ask your broker or bank to chase it up if you have not got one after two months.

## THE COMPANY CALENDAR

### Company news

The real things to watch for are announcements from your company.

10

The most important news points in a normal year are the interim profits statement, and the preliminary results for the year.

You cannot count on either of these crucial statements being sent to you. The Stock Exchange requires all shareholders to be treated equally, and companies are not allowed to give advance knowledge of any announcements to anyone. That is the theory, and quite right it is too. Unfortunately, in practice, some investors are more equal than others. All company announcements go to a Stock Exchange department first. Then they are displayed in the Stock Exchange, and flashed around the City on sophisticated and expensive electronic communications systems. All of the big investment houses, brokers and such have them. So they know any company news right away, and can buy and sell the shares long before the small shareholder gets a whiff of what is happening. Individual investors have to wait – and wait.

Almost all company news items are sent to the newspapers, but this does not mean that the news of your company will appear. The *Daily Mail*, for example, comments on only the most interesting items, while the *Financial Times* publishes almost all of them, sometimes two or three days late. It is hit or miss for individual investors. Only if the company itself posts news to them overnight, and delays announcing it to the Stock Exchange until the start of dealings on the next morning do smaller investors have anything like equal access to information. That, unhappily, rarely happens.

In practice, most companies do post interim reports to shareholders, but often they leave it for a week or two after the announcement to the Stock Exchange, printing them at leisure. It is daft. What small investors need is the news from the company at the same time as the big boys get it, never mind the glossy paper.

The interim report carries news of profits in the first half of the company's trading year, the amount of the interim dividend (a cheque for which may not be posted for weeks after the announcement) and perhaps a short note on progress. Most of it will have been forecast already by the stockbrokers who follow the company, and only a real surprise will prompt any great move in the share price. Quite often, share prices fall on good news. The snag here is that this will have already been widely anticipated by the City's backroom boys. They need something extra-special to be impressed further.

Preliminary profits for the full trading year are hardly ever sent direct to shareholders, though they are the most important news in a normal year. They are called 'preliminary' because often they are unaudited, but for practical purposes they are the real thing. They come with news of the dividend for the year, and perhaps a word or

11

two on the company's outlook. Once again, the sharks in the City usually see them before they filter through to individual investors.

## Company reports and accounts

Roughly three weeks after notice of the preliminary profits comes the company's report and accounts. This can be anything from a slim, austere booklet with little more than the legal minimum of information to a glossy 60-page effort, replete with colour photographs of the chairman, a statement of company philosophy and, perhaps, a few special offers of the company's products. Glossiness does not necessarily denote investment merit.

## The annual meeting

The accounts must give at least three weeks' notice of the time, place and date of the annual meeting. All Ordinary shareholders are entitled to attend, can ask questions and vote on a proposal or two. You can vote, even if you do not attend, as companies must send out proxy voting forms. The votes will normally cover the election of a few directors (some must be re-elected every few years), and will probably give the board freedom to issue new shares without consulting shareholders. Shareholders will also be asked to approve the payment of the final dividend for the year. (Interim dividends do not have to be approved by shareholders.) The chairman may well make a short statement on trading. Sometimes that will be sent to the press, but it will rarely be circulated by the company to those who miss the meeting. Shortly after, cheques for the final dividend will be posted.

That, then, is the company calendar – what you can expect in a normal year as a shareholder. Do not forget that it is *your* company: as a shareholder, you own a small piece of it. If you do not like what is going on, write to the chairman and tell him. Sensible comments should expect sensible answers.

# 3  Why Shares Rise and Fall

Share prices rise because there are more buyers than sellers, and fall when sellers outnumber buyers. That is the standard, half-mocking City reply from the chap who has seen prices move, and does not really know why. The answer may be correct, but tells you very little.

Quite often you can unearth no better explanation. Share prices frequently *appear* to move for no reason, because of nothing more than pure chance. In reality, they do not, of course. There is always a reason. It is simply that you have not been able to discover it.

Perhaps it was largely chance. The jobbers – the wholesalers in shares – may have marked the price down to generate a little interest, or because they saw a small seller, and no one wanted to buy. The seller may simply have wanted the cash for a new car, so the price change may have had absolutely no link to the company's fortunes.

On the other hand, if the seller is married to the brother of the company's sales manager, and the company has not told shareholders but it has just lost a large contract, then it might mean something. The sales manager's sister-in-law is not someone who means anything to anyone in the City. There is no restriction on her share dealing, as she is not quite an insider. Yet if she sells enough shares on a quiet day, she could move the price of even quite a large company.

Or perhaps a price moves because the jobber has a problem with another share he deals in and he may need extra cash. So he may cut the prices of a string of shares, simply in the hope of finding buyers and thus raising cash. Perhaps he could not manage *The Times* crossword, the train was late and he tripped coming up the stairs. In a rotten mood, he sees that the pound is falling, and decides to lower prices across the board. He feels better after lunch, and the pound is steadier, but no one has come in to buy, so he leaves them at the lower value.

No way to run a market, wiping millions of pounds off the value of public companies on a whim? Crazy and irresponsible? Perhaps. But it happens. You can never quite be sure why share prices move.

## WHAT OUGHT TO MAKE PRICES MOVE: THE BASIC RULES

None the less, there are certain ground-rules, basic items that do influence share prices. None of them has to be committed to heart; you can get by without knowing them. But others use them, and since playing the stock market is ultimately about anticipating what the next chap will do, and using it to your best advantage, they are worth thinking about.

Start with the report and accounts every company must send out each year. Because it is largely historical, a picture of where the company was at the end of the trading year, it is of limited value. Share prices are concerned about what happens next, but the past can yield clues to the future.

## THE COMPANY'S REPORT AND ACCOUNTS

A company's report and accounts is split into six main sections: the chairman's statement; the directors' report; the profit and loss account; the balance sheet; the statement of the source and application of funds; and the auditors' report.

*Why the chairman's statement matters*

The chairman's statement may be accompanied by a separate report from the managing director, or chief executive, and some companies publish ones from the managers of individual sections of the business. All of these may provide some idea of how things look in the current year, and they give a useful feel of what the company actually does. Note the names of the operating companies; there is usually a list of them. The names often bear no relationship to the name on your share certificate. Great Universal Stores, for example, owns Burberrys, Times Furnishing and mail-order giants such as Marshall Ward. And did you realize that Hanson Trust owns the Allders department stores and Ever Ready batteries? If you see them around, you may be able to judge what is going on in the company as a whole.

*The directors' report*

The directors' report tells you briefly what the company does, outlines changes in the company's structure – e.g. sales or purchases of important parts of the business – and lists how many shares the directors own (have a beneficial interest in), and how many they help

14

look after as trustees (non-beneficial). It should also show any changes since the last accounts, and may detail moves between the end of the trading year and the date of the report. In addition, it must list anyone who holds more than 5 per cent of the shares.

Obviously it is worth checking what the directors have been doing with their shares, and to see whether they control the company. A holding of 50 per cent or more gives absolute control, but anything over 30 per cent can usually be regarded as effective control. A holding such as this diminishes the chances of a takeover bid, unless some outsider has 29.9 per cent – which means a bid may be in the offing. If there are several outsiders with more than 5 per cent, or someone is building up a stake, there is more chance of a bid.

## The profit and loss account

The profit and loss account shows just how the profit or loss for the trading year was made up. The top line is usually turnover or sales (effectively the same thing). Then comes the cost of sales – a hefty figure that covers all the normal costs of running the business. Take the cost of sales away from the sales, and you are left with the trading (or gross) profit. Then there may be a share of profits, or losses, of related companies; these are results from businesses the main company does not own completely. Part of their profit will have to be deleted from the main company's total, because this belongs to the other shareholders in those companies. If the partly owned companies made losses, there will be a credit to the main company, representing the share of the losses to be borne by outside shareholders. These items are often called *minority interests*.

The next line normally shows interest charges or credits. If there is an employee profit-sharing scheme, the contribution to that will follow. Knock these off trading profits and you have pre-tax profits, the figure most widely quoted by the press.

The most important figure for serious investors, though, is net profit after tax, and after paying any preference dividends. Because of capital allowances, past losses and such, the tax charge might sometimes be low. Until recently, analysts used to base their sums on profits after a theoretical full tax charge, reasoning that to compare one company with another, they should not take notice of tax charges that might vary from year to year. Now, however, most people look at the published net profit figures, after the tax is actually paid.

Net profits show the amount available to pay dividends and the next line in the account gives the cost of paying whatever dividend the directors recommend. In practice, dividends do not always cost what the accounts say, but that need not bother you. What is left after paying dividends is available to be transferred to reserves, where it can be used to expand the business. The bigger the reserves, the better, so long as shareholders receive a decent dividend.

Some profit and loss accounts show *earnings per share*, one of the most widely used figures in investment. This is calculated by dividing the profits after tax and preference dividends (sometimes known as *net attributable profits*, or *profits attributable to Ordinary shareholders*) by the number of Ordinary shares in issue.

For example, take a company with profits after tax and preference dividends of £500,000, with 1 million £1 shares in issue. That company has earnings per share of 50p. Then divide the earnings per share into the share price, and you arrive at the *price/earnings ratio*. Say the shares of the company are selling at 450p, the price/earnings ratio would be 9 (450p divided by 50p).

The price/earnings ratio – sometimes simply called the PE ratio – is the most widely used of all investment tools. Sometimes people say a share is selling at so many times, or so many years, earnings. In a way, that description is the most graphic. It illustrates how many years it would take to earn net profits equal to the stock market value of the company.

You will not, however, find the price/earnings ratio in your report and accounts. It would be misleading for a company to report it, because it changes with each move in the shares, rising as the price rises and falling as it drops.

*The balance sheet*

The next major section in the report and accounts is the balance sheet. This is effectively a snap-shot of what the company owned and owed at the trading year-end. The assets are listed first. There are fixed assets: land, buildings, plant, machinery and so on. And there are current assets: investments, stocks, cash and debtors. The bigger the assets, the better. Check the date on which the fixed assets were last valued. Most properties rise in value, and their true worth may be understated if there has not been a revaluation recently. Look at plant, machinery and stock values more sceptically. Outdated plant and machinery may not be saleable at the balance sheet value, and if a company gets caught with a lot of stock that has declined in value, that is bad news. There will also be a figure for creditors, covering the money the company has to pay out within a year. This could include overdrafts and, perhaps, tax bills. Subtract creditors from current assets, and you get net current assets – or net current liabilities if the short-term debts exceed the quickly realizable assets.

Next the balance sheet adds fixed assets and net current assets (or takes away net current liabilities). Then it subtracts other liabilities – the money the company owes but can leave for a year or more. These generally include large loans that run for a fixed number of years before repayment. Take one from the other, and you have the net asset value of the business – theoretically the price you would get if you shut up shop and sold out. The greater the excess of assets over liabilities, the richer the company, especially if the assets are strong in cash or saleable property.

Beneath this comes a section showing how it is all financed, through capital and reserves. There will be the amount of paid-up share capital, covering the preference shares and Ordinary shares in issue, taken at their nominal, or par, value. Then there are reserves, what has been left over through the years from profits after tax and dividends. Put them together, and they are known as *shareholders' funds*. Some market men pay close attention to the proportion of debt to shareholders' funds – what is called the *gearing*. The higher the proportion of borrowing goes, the more they worry.

## Source and application of funds

All accounts carry a section on the source and application of funds. This shows where cash has come from through the year, and where it went. Coming in, there will be profits, depreciation (the money the company sets aside for wear-and-tear on machinery and other fixed assets), asset sales and borrowings. Going out there will be the cost of paying dividends, tax and buying companies. It is a simple guide, and worth checking.

## The auditors' report

Somewhere in the whole shebang will be a modest, but vital section – the auditors' report. Normally this is a few brief lines, certifying that the financial statements give a true and fair view of the state of affairs and conform to the Companies Act. A glance will suffice, if that is the message, which it will be for most companies. If it differs, then watch out.

Strictly speaking, the auditors are accountants employed by shareholders to verify that the directors are running the business in accordance with the law, to see that the figures are what the report and accounts say they are. If necessary, they send out warnings to shareholders, but only through a stilted code: the accounts are

17

normally presented on a going-concern basis, which means things are well; if there is any qualification to that phrase, it can be a serious matter.

The auditors may say that continued operation as a going concern depends on further finance, or the continuation of existing loan facilities by the bankers. That means the company could be in trouble unless someone puts more money in, or if the bank decides to call in the overdraft. If the auditors are unable to form an opinion as to whether the accounts give a true and fair view, sell your shares at once. They are saying something is badly wrong.

Almost any qualification is serious, but one or two can be shrugged off. Sometimes companies do not conform to some recommended accounting rule and the auditors are obliged to draw attention to this, but they may well agree that it does not matter. Then they will say that, in spite of the variation, the accounts do give a true and fair view.

One further point: check who the auditors are. Big names are by no means infallible, but they can generally be taken more seriously than a local firm who may not have other lucrative public company accounts to audit. Directors do lean on auditors . . . and sometimes auditors bend.

## SCANNING THE FINE PRINT

You may think that this sounds enough – more than enough – for a company report and accounts. However, there is more, and when you really get into the investment game, you will be glad of it. All accounts have several pages of notes, amplifying and explaining the profit and loss account. And there will be a statement of accounting policy, talking about the basis of valuation, the rate at which machinery is written off (depreciation) and so on.

### Depreciation

Depreciation can be important. Take two transport companies. Company 1 may write down lorries by 25 per cent a year, setting aside that amount against profits, but Company 2 may write off the lorries at 20 per cent a year. So profits from Company 1 appear to be lower than Company 2's for the first four years. Of course, Company 1 may be able to run the lorries for five years. If their value has been written down to nil after four years, Year 5 requires no depreciation, and profits benefit sharply. Company 2 which will have shown higher profits in Years 1 to 4, will still be writing off the lorries in Year 5, so profits will then lag by comparison. It is usually not that simple in real life, but depreciation does matter.

### Extraordinary items

Notes to the accounts will also show any extraordinary items, such as exceptional sales that have boosted the profits, or heavy redundancies or write-offs holding them back. Sometimes it is possible to predict a big profit swing simply by the absence of one-off charges or credits in the following year.

## SCRIP ISSUES

Once you have worked through a report and accounts, and struck up a nodding acquaintance with the mysteries within, you are well on the way to completing an elementary crib on the coarse art of investment analysis. There are, however, a few more items which crop up fairly frequently. Scrip issues are the most welcome.

The scrip issue comes under several different names – a capitalization issue, a share bonus or a free scrip issue. It is called a free scrip issue because it hands out shares which no one has to pay for. Strictly speaking, it is merely a sophisticated piece of book-keeping. A company with a fistful of reserves transforms them into extra shares, which it gives to its owners – the shareholders.

In reality, nothing is given away. All that happens is that the nominal capital increases, and everyone has more shares. In theory, the company itself is not worth a penny more, so the share price should simply be adjusted to reflect the capital change. If there has been a one-for-one bonus, giving every shareholder twice the number of shares they had before, the price should halve. Nothing gained, nothing lost.

Psychologically, however, the impact is valuable, and shareholders know it. Time and again at annual meetings, it is the one thing small shareholders care about: 'Please, Mr Chairman, can we have a scrip issue?' Good luck to them. News of plans for a scrip issue usually sends shares higher, and they may rise again just before the new shares are given out, and yet again after they are issued. It is an important sign of corporate confidence.

Take shares trading at 400p. On news of a one-for-one scrip, they might rise to 405p. Ahead of the actual issue, they might hit 420p. After the issue, the price is halved to take account of the new shares, and then the shares might pop up to 215p – equivalent to 430p before it all started. Wonderful what corporate paper-shuffling can do.

Everyone likes more for their money. It feels better to buy 500 shares at 200p each than to buy 250 at 400p, or 100 at £10 a time. When shares get too high, the market frowns. Anything over 400p is heavy, and heavy is not so much fun. There is a whole band of investors who only buy 'penny' stocks – that is, shares selling at under £1 (a penny gets you nowhere these days). A scrip issue suits them. It cuts the share price down to size.

### Share splits

Occasionally, companies achieve a similar effect by splitting their capital. Shares with a nominal value of £1 might be split into two shares of 50p, or ten of 10p. Again, the change is cosmetic, but it leaves the company looking more attractive.

## RIGHTS ISSUES

A rights issue is rather different as it involves the sale of new shares to existing shareholders. It is a way of raising cash, giving all investors an equal chance to join in, if they wish.

It can be a mixed blessing. Some shareholders will be unwilling, or unable, to buy new shares, so to ensure that they get their cash, most companies arrange underwriting. Banks and brokers agree to buy or find buyers for the rights shares in return for a small commission. Normally, rights shares are sold about 20 per cent below the market price, and if the market price falls beneath the rights price, the underwriters step in and take up the shares.

Some companies go for a *deep-discount* rights issue, pricing the new shares way below the market. This is to make them appear an irresistible bargain so that there is no need to incur the cost of underwriting. It is just a piece of sly company PR. What matters is how much the company is trying to raise, and whether it is perceived to be a good idea. But a deep-discounted rights issue is usually a helpful sign of confidence.

Most rights issues are sweetened by forecasts of higher profits and dividends to help offset the adverse impact of extra shares. If a rights issue flops and much of it is left with underwriters, the failure can dog the share price for months, even years. The market will be awash with shares, and every time the price perks up, it is likely to be hit by selling from the underwriters.

There is no rule that says shareholders have to take up their rights. It may be best not to. Some rights issues are a sign that a company is in trouble, needing extra cash to carry on, though the issue will not be presented that way. You lose nothing by refusing the shares. Leave them alone, and because the company is growing larger, issuing more shares, you will be left with a smaller proportion of the capital, a smaller piece of the cake.

If the rights terms are judged correctly, others will be willing to buy the new shares you do not want. You should then be able to sell the rights to your new shares for a small premium. Calculating the premium is complicated, but brokers or bankers will have it at their fingertips, simply by checking the market price. In some cases, you can sell part of your rights, and use the profit to buy a few of the new shares.

The kind of rights issue you want is one from a smallish company under new management. It is a standard ploy for ambitious company promoters to buy into a sleepy company, and raise new capital by a rights issue. I explain how to handle this later in the book.

Rights issues can be good news in bigger companies, too. The reputation and skills of the directors are what matters. The share price may take a while to settle down, but sometimes simply using the new cash to cut borrowings can have a dramatic impact on profits. Or the money may be used to buy exciting new businesses.

# 4 How Does the Market Work?

Your basic share jungle survival kit in place, next find your jungle. Where do you go to buy and sell the shares to make your killing?

There is still nowhere to beat the Stock Exchange. Housed in one of the great grey tower blocks sitting in Throgmorton Street, slap in the middle of the City, close by the Bank of England and the Mansion House, the London Stock Exchange is still where most of the action happens. News film of the familiar six-sided boxes on the trading floor flash regularly on the TV screens. And you can still wander into the visitors' gallery to watch the dealers buzzing below, and listen to a charming lady explaining what might be going on.

## THE BIG BANG

These days, though, the Stock Exchange tower is under siege. In October 1986, it was hit by the Big Bang, the loudest explosion in the Exchange's 200-year history. The impact is still rattling around the City.

Before the Big Bang, only Stock Exchange members could buy and sell shares on the Stock Exchange, only UK firms could provide members and members all charged the same fixed rates of commission for dealing. If you wanted to buy, you had to use a stockbroker. (If you bought through your bank, your bank used a broker.) The broker had to go to a stockjobber, who could not deal with the public, only with brokers. Jobbers determined share prices: they would mark them up when they had more buyers and down when there were more sellers.

If that systems sounds rather cosy, with everyone nicely protected from the fiercer winds of competition, that is exactly how it seemed to Sir Gordon Borrie at the Office of Fair Trading. He huffed and puffed, and forced the Stock Exchange to agree to changes. Those changes sparked the Big Bang, and were far more radical than Stock Exchange members expected when they decided not to battle against Borrie through the courts.

## INSIDER TRADING

On the whole, the old system did work fairly well. The split between brokers and jobbers actually stopped too much jiggery-pokery on share prices.

It was not perfect. Almost any trading system offers opportunities for those in the know to tilt things their way. The worst abuse came from something that still goes on – insider trading. The insider uses privileged information to buy and sell shares before everyone else knows what it going on. It is illegal, but tough to prove. The few court cases so far have been against the tiddlers, little operators who got careless. The syndicates of big money professionals, making millions from the advance information which comes to them in the course of earning their daily bread, survive unscathed so far.

Anyone who ventures into the stock market has to accept this as one of the facts of life. Distinguishing insider trading from intelligent, well-informed trading is well-nigh impossible. No one buys or sells a share without thinking they know better than the other chap. For every buyer, there is a seller. It is the capitalist system in the raw. If it upsets you, keep out of the stock market.

Unhappily, the Big Bang may not have made the system any kinder to the individual investor. Now, whoever you ask to buy shares for you may be working for the very firm which sells them to you. They could even be working for the giant financial supermarket, the kind of operation which seeks to offer all things financial to all people, which may have floated the company originally, may handle their take-over bids and may even hold the board's hand all day, every day.

A wonderful array of rules and regulations have been introduced to prevent any possible cheating. Elaborate safeguards have been erected to cut off one part of the supermarket from the other. City superstars are required to blank off parts of their brains, allowing nothing to spill over from one deal to another. And into the middle of all of this have barged big-money foreigners, used to different rules and customs, and sometimes more ruthlessly dedicated to the pursuit of profit. The Japanese may still be a relatively unknown quantity, but hard experience suggests that the Americans, at least, play a much tougher, nastier game than the City establishment.

23

Only time will tell how it works. However, the new system resembles the one the government forced the Lloyd's insurance market to abandon after hundreds of millions of pounds were stolen by highly skilled and well-respected members.

Do not let all of this dismay you. The individual investor will not be trampled under foot. But you should tread carefully – it can be dangerous out there in Throgmorton Street.

## WHERE TO BUY

Alerted yet undeterred by this alarmist stuff, where do you actually go to get on with it? There are three ways of buying or selling shares: through a member of the Stock Exchange, through a bank or through a licensed dealer in securities.

*Stockbrokers*

Stockbrokers – that is, members of the Stock Exchange – are much your best bet. Their conduct is covered by the rules of the Stock Exchange. If they should go bust (or be 'hammered' in Stock Exchange terms), or you can prove that they have cost you money by breaking the rules, there is a Stock Exchange compensation fund to pay up. 'My Word Is My Bond' is the Stock Exchange motto, and it counts: most stockbrokers are honourable, and will handle your affairs carefully and correctly. Their advice requires greater caution. Most give honest, well-meaning advice, but the small investor cannot reasonably expect to command too much of the time, nor perhaps the attention, of the most skilled and experienced brokers.

Different services are developing. Since the Big Bang, some brokers offer a no-frills, discount dealing service: they will simply execute your share-trading instructions, charging a modest commission, without giving advice. Others will manage your money, send regular portfolio valuations and so on, and allow you access to their research and investment ideas, but this may be too costly for the small investor. In the middle, there are firms offering a little advice, perhaps cheap dealing in certain circumstances, with extra charges for special facilities.

As a rule, you will find it cheaper to deal with one of the brokers outside London. Lower overheads allow them to charge less, and they may have more time for individual investors. On the other hand, they may not be quite so well in touch with the action – if that is what you want.

Many brokers will try to persuade investors with £20,000 or less to put their money into unit trusts. It makes some sense (*see* p.3), but takes the excitement out of investment. If you are reading this book, you want to play the share game for yourself.

Even £20,000 may be too little for some big London brokers to love you. Most want at least £50,000, and preferably £100,000 before they will manage a share portfolio. Some add charges for valuation, or for safe-keeping of share certificates, plus an annual management fee. The best will be worth the expense, and will supply advice over a wide range, from income tax to capital gains tax and inheritance tax.

Finding a good broker is not easy. Ideally, you want someone you can trust and confide in, with a minute or two to talk when you need it. Personal recommendation is best, but you can only really judge how a broker suits you by working with him. If things do not click, go elsewhere – it is your money at stake. Brokers are salespeople acting on your behalf; *you* are the boss. (*See also* p.86)

Watch the financial press for advertisements. Then ask anyone whom you think might know about the firm of your choice. A big name may not be enough. Some of the big boys are super, but you may not be big enough to matter to them, even with £100,000. You could find yourself in the care of some fresh-faced graduate, learning the business. He may mean well, but he may not manage too well.

If you cannot find a broker by other means, the Stock Exchange will refer you to one willing to take on new clients. The Exchange also sends out an excellent free booklet 'An Introduction to the Stock Market.' Ask for it. Contact the Secretary at one of the addresses listed at the end of the book, or contact the Public Information Department, The Stock Exchange, London EC2N 1HP.

## Using your bank

If you are not happy about using a stockbroker, you might feel more comfortable with your bank. In the past, this has not been something to recommend. Banks simply dealt through stockbrokers, and usually added a charge of £5.00, a system that was more expensive and more ponderous than using a broker direct – for example, it could take a day for a bank's instructions to be carried out by a broker – and the banks were not equipped to give much advice.

That is changing. Banks are involved in the new financial supermarkets, and are promising to pep up their services. Some branches are to get faster dealing facilities and screens showing share prices, and will be making a real effort to help. Try it and see, but do not expect your local manager to become a share whizz-kid, or to provide the cheapest service.

*The licensed dealers*

The third way into the share market is through a licensed dealer in securities. These were licensed by the Department of Trade, which has passed supervision of them to the Financial Intermediaries, Managers and Brokers Regulatory Association (FIMBRA) and, ultimately, to the Securities and Investment Board. They have to follow certain rules, but these are not as tough, nor as carefully policed, as those for members of the Stock Exchange. And there is no central compensation fund.

Several of the most widely advertised licensed dealers have attracted a lot of flak in recent years. They advertise in the financial press whenever there is an exciting new issue, offering to deal free of commission. However, nobody offers anything for nothing: to cover their costs, they give slightly less favourable buying and selling prices than on the Stock Exchange. This is not necessarily more expensive, and for many small investors, trading a new issue through a licensed dealer will be clean and easy.

## THE OVER-THE-COUNTER MARKET

Take care, though. The more prominent licensed dealers also trade in the Over-The-Counter (OTC) market. There is no counter, and many would claim there is no real market. The OTC market exists on the telephone, and trades shares in companies too small, too risky or too new to make it on the Stock Exchange. Some have fine prospects, and some graduate to the main markets; others are appalling. Many have been launched by the OTC market-makers themselves. They may not meet Stock Exchange disclosure standards, and it may be extremely hard to sell their shares, though it is usually easy to buy them. Some companies have gone under amid accusations that the OTC dealers were recommending them when they must have known they were in trouble.

The message is clear. If you deal through a licensed dealer, do not buy anything he or she recommends unless you are certain about it. Any shares that are only traded on the OTC market will be riskier than you imagine. There are bargains, but it takes a very experienced – or very lucky – investor to spot them.

Some licensed dealers will try to sell you shares in fully quoted companies. They may be fine, they may not be. The dealers may have bought a large number of them at below the listed price. They then try to sell them on in small lots at higher prices, hoping to make a profit along the way. There is nothing wrong in this, but sometimes

26

they cause the price on the main market to rise higher, making those they are selling appear more of a bargain. Be wary.

There are some perfectly reputable licensed dealers. It is only when the hard sell starts that their interest in making a living can operate against your interest in making a good investment.

Whenever you do use a licensed dealer, give no indication as to whether you want to buy or sell when you call. Simply ask the price of the share, and the number of shares he or she will trade in. If you reveal that you want to buy, the dealers may raise the price they quote you. If you show you are a seller, the price may be reduced. And do try to haggle.

## THE THIRD-TIER MARKET

The new Third-Tier market has been feeling its way inside the Stock Exchange since autumn 1986. It is designed to take in the over-the-counter stocks, and to bring a welcome element of uniformity and regulation to the more speculative end of the market, though this will still be for gamblers only. Sensibly, the shares traded on the Third-Tier carry a wealth warning to ward off widows and orphans, but it has potential as a place to launch start-up companies and others which do not qualify for the senior markets. Treat it with caution.

As the new City Big Bang regulations come into play, however, the Third-Tier market is likely to become the home of many or all of the licensed dealers. If it does, they will have been forced into a more formally regulated system than prevailed before. That will be a good thing, and may make them safer to deal with – though, inevitably, trading with some of them will still require considerable care and a dash of nerve.

## THE UNLISTED SECURITIES MARKET

The Unlisted Securities Market (USM) exists already, between the full market and the Third-Tier market. It was set up in November 1980 to cater for companies that do not qualify for a full listing. However, the market does not exist separately; all USM shares are traded on the main market. USM companies only need a three-year trading record to qualify (compared to five on the full market), and can sell a smaller amount of their capital.

USM issues are more speculative than fully listed companies, and it can be difficult to deal in the shares freely. American companies are beginning to come to London on the USM; some are fine companies, but be careful. Prices move especially erratically, and because they are not based here, the flow of news is not always good, and the shares can drift lower through lack of interest.

## SHARE SHOPS

Share shops attract a lot of attention, but take care. They may be handy, unstuffy places to go, where you will feel comfortable chatting to someone face to face about shares, but that can be dangerous. It is harder to say no to some friendly fellow sitting opposite you than to a distant voice on the telephone. It is also tempting to take decisions on the spur of the moment, with a little prompting from the expert at your elbow.

It is best to ask advice at the share shop, take it away and mull it over. Go back later to trade, if you wish. Spending several hundred pounds on shares is not to be taken lightly; it is not like an impulse buy, a packet of crisps at the cash register.

Share shops vary. Check who is behind them. Stockbrokers Quilter Goodison, the firm headed by Stock Exchange chairman Sir Nicholas Goodison, have led the way and are trustworthy, sensible people. Other stockbroking firms will follow, and when you trade with them, you trade with the security of Stock Exchange rules around you.

Other share shops may be owned by licensed dealers, and lack this safety net. They may be well-run and respectable, but all sorts of organizations may set up as share shops. Check who they are, and what guarantees of security they can give. Do not be blinded by smiles and smooth talk. A salesman is there to sell to you; make sure you are getting exactly what you want before you buy.

## DEALING COSTS

Share-dealing costs have been thrown into confusion by the end of fixed commission rules in the Big Bang, and are still settling down. Brokers used to charge a minimum £10 for a purchase, and £7 for a sale; many, though, set a minimum of £15 or £25 on small deals. On deals under £7000 the minimum commission was 1.65 per cent, falling as trades got bigger. Still remaining is the inevitable 15 per cent VAT on the commission charge, with (from 27 October 1986) stamp duty at 0.5 per cent on purchases, nothing on sales. There is also a 60p contract stamp, and there could be some modest levy to cover the costs of the assorted new regulatory bodies which come into being around Big Bang time.

There is a new system that should go some way towards reducing dealing costs and time, and should be ready before the end of 1987. This is SAEF, an incomprehensible set of initials which stands for 'SEAQ [Stock Exchange Automated Quotations] Automatic Execution Facility'. This little lot is the brain-child of the Stock Exchange. When the computers are working, it should allow trades in up to 1000 shares at a time in the biggest companies to be executed automatically on a screen. Press the button, and the best price in that share at that moment will be guaranteed. Hopefully, that could cut dealing costs on such a trade to £5 or so a time. We shall see.

## ACCOUNT TRADING

The Stock Exchange trading calendar is divided into time periods called *accounts*. These are normally two weeks long, or three weeks around bank holidays. All bills are settled on the Monday, ten days after the account ends. If you buy a share and sell it within the account, you pay only one set of broker's commission. So short-term in-and-out dealing costs less.

It also opens the magical vista of making a profit without actually putting any cash down. If you buy and sell in the account at a profit, your broker simply sends a cheque for your winnings. Buy and sell at a loss, and you send your broker a cheque.

Account trading is very risky. You need a volatile share price, good judgement and fine timing. You not only have to make enough to cover the (reduced) dealing cost, but also to cover the jobber's turn. Whereas the financial press quotes the middle price of a share, when you actually trade you discover there is a difference between the buying and selling price – the jobber's turn or market-maker's profit. He will buy, say, Marks & Spencer for 190p, or sell at 194p; the price in the newspaper will be 192p, the middle price.

It might appear that when the shares rise to 197p in the account, you are making a profit. Sadly, it is not so simple. When the middle price was 192p, you would have bought your Marks & Spencer share at 194p. With the middle price at 197p, the jobber would actually be quoting 195p for him to buy (the bid price) and 199p to sell (the offer price). So you would only be able to sell for 195p, and thus would only be 1p ahead *before* costs. In practice, you need to be able to get 197p simply to break even *after* costs. That means a middle price of 199p, a rise of 7p.

Trading in the account is much tougher than it first appears. It is not a good thing to indulge in unless you have lots of spare cash, an iron nerve and instant access to a broker who will trade quickly and shrewdly for you.

Banish such dreams for the while. They do help show, however, how the costs of share dealing work.

The Big Bang has thrown the system into disarray. Some will offer discount dealing, others will charge more and offer frills. The scene is changing fast. Keep the old commission scales in mind as a guide to what is reasonable. Welcome to the capitalist class.

# 5 The Economy and All That Jazz

Now that you know roughly what you are getting when you buy a share, and where you can buy it, is this the time to get on with it?

Sorry to introduce such a disturbing notion when you are bursting to put your new-found investment skills into practice, but timing is crucial to successful dealing. Knowing when to buy and when to sell is almost more important than knowing what to buy. And when you are judging timing, it is best to start with the big picture – the macro-economic scene, in modern jargon.

The memory of the secondary banking collapse and the mayhem it created in the stock market lingers in the minds of City folk over the age of 40. It helps explain why so many of the successful fund managers of the 1980s are not yet out of their 20s: these people are not inhibited by what happened last time it all went *phut*. They do not need to shake off the ghost of 1974, when share prices plummeted, and left even our biggest and best businesses rated as if they were on the way to the knacker's yard. Thankfully, all but a few survived, and shares have soared since, providing a wonderful base for a bull market which really began to roar from the summer of 1985.

The 1974 collapse broke many an ace share punter. And everyone knows how the Great Crash of 1929 laid the United States low, and dragged on into the depression of the 1930s. The 1890s were pretty tough, too. In May 1866, the collapse of the Overend Gurney Company triggered a stock market slump in London, hard on the heels of a financial panic and banking collapse which had roared across Europe and the United States in the preceding two years. And so it goes, back to the South Sea Bubble in 1720 and earlier.

Sometimes, it seems, you just cannot get it right. The glittering prizes are torn away, and supershares become dogs overnight. In a major collapse, the stock market is no place to be, unless you are a brilliant bear. Bears sell shares they do not own in the hope of buying them back at a lower price later. It is not a game for the small

31

investor. To play it successfully, you need iron nerves, and a bank balance to match.

When the stock market slumps, either get out fast, and sit on your cash – time for the building societies or the National Savings Investment Bank – or grit your teeth and hang on. Most shares are all right in the long run, and when the market does turn, it can turn hard and fast.

You can never be quite sure how long the turn will take, what changes there will be in your circumstances along the way, whether you will need your money suddenly or whether you are holding shares in the odd company which will go bust. It is a sad, sorry wait to watch and hope your shares will clamber back to what you paid – and never mind about inflation.

In the end, you cannot buck the trend. And it is because you need to have some idea of what sets the trend that you should take a deep breath and worry a little about the economy, inflation, the petro-pound and all that jazz. You cannot ignore them. The City can be mesmerized by such things, and it is the big City money – and, increasingly, the big bucks from Wall Street and Japan – which ultimately determines which way the market moves.

Lock 100 economists in a room, and you will start a riot. When it is over, there will be 100 different views of how the economy is faring and where it is going. If they arrive at something approaching agreement, they have got it wrong, be they ever so clever. The individual investor cannot hope to get it right, except in the broadest of terms – and that is all that matters.

The basic decision you should take is whether the economy is going up, sideways or down, and whether that is likely to change soon. Share prices are largely determined by what people think will happen next. Knowing what is happening now helps, and what happened last year matters a little, but the crystal ball stuff counts most. Your guess may be as good as anyone else's.

## PROFITS AND DIVIDENDS FIRST

Strip away the mumbo-jumbo, and what matters to a share price is profits, and the dividend those profits will pay. Capital gains are great – and the prospect of capital gains is what attracts investors to shares instead of to the building societies or some other fixed-interest holding – but the dividend is what matters in the end. Dividends certainly matter to the big players – the pension funds and insurance companies. They buy shares for a long-term stream of income to cover their future liabilities.

## THE REVERSE YIELD GAP

The *reverse yield gap* is one of the most common bits of jargon used in discussing dividend yields (dividend yields are the amount a share pays you in dividends each year for every £100 you have invested). In the late 1950s, investors woke up to the fact that shares were a better bet than fixed-interest stocks, because shares could produce capital gains as well as a dividend. Fixed-interest investments just paid out a dividend (interest), while their capital was eaten away by inflation. When you sold them, your capital was worth much less than when you put it in. The view had been that, because shares moved up and down in value, they were more risky than fixed-interest investments, and so needed to give a higher return in dividends (interest). Then the idea dawned that, if shares could bring capital gains which would compensate for the decline in capital brought about by inflation, perhaps a lower return (dividend yield) on shares than on fixed-interest investments was acceptable.

The whole basis of investment went into reverse. In 1959, yields on fixed-interest government securities rose above those on shares for the first time. The reverse yield gap came into being – the difference between what government securities return, and what the average share yields.

Profits influence dividends, which in turn influence share prices. So what matters in the economy for the investor is whatever influences profits. That means almost anything, and almost anything can be interpreted as good or bad, depending on the City's mood.

## INFLATION

Inflation is one of the crucial elements. In the 1960s, investors approved of inflation at 2 or 3 per cent a year: it kept profits moving ahead on paper. Come the 1970s, with inflation over 25 per cent, and everyone changed their minds. High inflation means that money for buying new plant and machinery costs too much, so new investment to generate extra profits is postponed. The customer has less to spend, so demand falls. Companies may report high profits, but they are worth less. Now, low inflation is universally approved. It is seen as establishing a secure base on which the economy can grow, and helping to keep costs in check against those of other countries where inflation may (wishful thinking) be higher. And there is a powerful lobby arguing that profits are worth more in times of low inflation and, because they are more secure, justify higher ratings for shares.

## THE EXCHANGE RATE

The pound plays a major role in influencing the level of inflation, and it also determines whether our exports are competitive around the world. A low pound makes our goods cheaper overseas, so big exporters do well. Companies with large overseas operations also look better, as their overseas profits become worth more when translated into sterling. It also means, however, that companies which rely on imports have to pay more, and their costs are consequently pushed higher. A low pound, then, tends to increase the rate of inflation. National pride can also combine with economic expediency by prompting politicians to raise interest rates to attract more money to prevent the pound falling further, all of which adds to inflationary pressures.

## INTEREST RATES

Higher interest rates are bad news for the economy and share prices. They raise the cost of money, which raises the cost of investing in new projects, plant and machinery and jobs, which would help bring the growth in production which we all want. And they raise the cost of the credit which provides an ever-greater proportion of the money we are spending in shops. That, in turn, feeds back to reduced orders for industry, so there is less overtime pay for people to spend, more jobs are lost, and so the downward spiral of economic activity goes on.

## OIL

Then, of course, we have oil – and sterling as the once-mighty petropound. Late 1985 and early 1986 saw a magical reversal of City attitudes as oil-fearing economists stood on their heads. When oil sold at $30 a barrel, the pound was riding high against other currencies. As an important oil producer, one of our major raw materials was not having to be bought overseas, and could even be exported, so our balance of payments – the amount we get in from other countries against the amount we spend overseas – looked relatively good. Fears that the oil price would fall to $25 a barrel began to unsettle sterling, sparking worries that the pound might plunge, and we might be forced to raise interest rates, thus strangling economic growth.

The City and the stock market had some desperately uneasy moments. Then it happened: the price of oil began to fall, and fall fast. By spring 1986, it had touched $10 a barrel, and few were prepared to predict an early rally. Suddenly, the stock market was racing ahead, catching everyone unprepared. All at once, cheaper oil was in fashion. The government had endured a nail-biting week or two, teetering on the brink of slamming interest rates up to prevent a plunge in the pound, and sterling had held up. And one economist after another saw the light – cheap oil was good for Britain, after all.

Just as dearer oil had brought the Western economies grinding to a halt in the Seventies, so cheaper oil would set them bopping ahead in the Eighties. Cheaper oil meant lower inflation, and would reduce costs so widely that it would be equivalent to an unofficial tax cut for everyone. And, the story ran, Britain, petropound or no, would ultimately benefit more from her role as an international trader than she would lose as an oil producer. Isn't economics wonderful?

That is a classic illustration of the folly of paying too much attention to economists. Yet it does show how important the economy itself and what everyone thinks about it can be to share traders. The stock market boom early in 1986 was due largely to the change in views on oil, yet the economic forecasts had read it all wrong until then.

What matters most is spotting a change of mood. Obviously if you hold share in companies which own shops and consumer spending figures slump, there will be a fall in those shares – for a while. Only if those gloomy spending figures are repeated a few times and it becomes clear that spending has turned well and truly down will there be a sustained slump. Again, if wholesale prices start soaring, and monthly figures for average earnings rocket month after month, a squeeze on company profit margins will develop: unless the retail price index soars even faster, watch out! However, you need not pore over such statistics too carefully. The backroom boys in the City will spot them first, and they will be reflected in share prices before you can do too much about it.

So the economy and all that jazz does matter – but only in the broadest sense. You could worry your life away trying to analyse government gobbledygook, and end up more confused than ever. And then, perhaps, you would realize that almost all government statistics are quietly revised later, and were way out first time around. If you look hard enough, the revisions themselves are revised much later. In truth, we are all adrift. No one has more than a rough idea of where we are going. And a rough idea of what is happening to the economy is all that really matters to most investors.

# 6 New Issues: Picking Pennies Off a Plate

It is 7.30 on a chill winter's morning. Already queues are forming outside a grey City bank. The office juniors are there, each with a thick wad of papers under his arm. Old ladies, with plastic bags bulging, chat to porters from the meat market. The odd City gent, velvet collar and brolly, reads his *Financial Times* alongside the men in long black coats and beards, guarding crammed cardboard boxes beside them on the pavement. A few characters are frantically scribbling on forms and writing cheques. Secretaries join the line as the police shepherd it away from the edge of the pavement, and the press photographer clicks away.

By 10 o'clock, with the bank doors long open, the queue has become a scrum, with sheaves of paper being shuffled out from hand to hand, and sleek City brokers directing office boys as they push through the crowd, throwing bundles across the bank counter into wicker baskets. At one minute past ten, the bank cries 'Time!', cashiers slam down the barriers across the counter and the commissionaires move to close the doors.

Another successful new issue is on its way, application lists closed, 10.01 a.m., heavily oversubscribed. Cheques worth hundreds of millions of pounds, much of it borrowed money, have poured into the bank, chasing shares in the latest stock market rave. Later that day, the lucky ones should know how many shares they have got. A week or so later, there will be a scramble as the Stock Exchange opens dealings, and the lucky winners rush to cash in their instant profits.

## STAGGING

It is all part of the great City game of stagging – buying shares in a new issue, hoping to sell at a hefty profit as soon as the shares hit the market. From the £200 punter up to the syndicate which puts up £100 million, it is a gambling bonanza which leaves Las Vegas standing and the bookmakers limping way down the field. One burly City broker counted his stagging profits in the tens of millions in 1985. Dozens of groups of fund managers, brokers, bankers and boys about the City worked more discreetly, and got together to make similar fortunes. In a matter of minutes, they scooped more profit than the average British company can earn in a year of hard slog.

The new-issue game is the nearest you will get to a free lunch in the City. Two million tried it with British Telecom in the autumn of 1984. All they had to do was fill in a form, write a cheque, take it to the bank or post it off, and sit back and wait for the profits to pour in. For every pound they put up, they had a profit of 86p in the first day of trading, and a few months later, they had £1.40 profit for every pound. Oh, the joys of the capitalist classes.

Telecom was an exception, of course. The government was determined to make it work. They spent millions promoting it, simplified the whole procedure and – if you listen to the political opposition – deliberately pitched the price too low and threw away hundreds of millions of taxpayers' money.

What about the Laura Ashley issue, then? Anyone could see that this was a good thing: shops booming all over Britain and in France, and plans to break into the United States. No political meddling there, just a good solid, commercial company, floating on the stock market to help unlock cash for the family, and raise more for future growth. Every share you bought at 135p could have been sold at 185p on the first day of dealing.

An exception? Not at all. In 1985, new issues galore roared off to a handsome profit in first-time dealings. One or two had their sticky moments, but they were few and far between. Anyone who stagged almost any new issue made a killing.

Something for nothing hardly sounds the way the City normally works, but so long as the stock market is in good-to-average form, making money on new issues is like picking pennies off a plate. The only problem is elbowing aside all of the others scrambling for the pickings, too, and making sure that you get your share – or more.

Because the new-issue system is geared to success, your friendly issuing house really needs you, big punter or small, when the action starts. A good issue is one which gives something to everyone, leaving them all feeling sweet. No banker or broker worth his salt aims to squeeze the last penny out of a new issue. If a company starts stock market life at a discount, a cloud may hang over it for years. Expansion plans are inhibited, and goodwill is gone. If you lose money backing a new issue, the sponsors have failed, not you – though that is little consolation for your bank balance.

37

# THE IDEAL WAY INTO SHARES

For anyone new to share trading, subscribing for a new issue is the ideal way into the market. You pay no stockbroking commission, no VAT, no stamp duty and no jobber's turn, and there are no hidden extras. The price you pay is the one on the application form. You do not even have to use a stockbroker, bank or licensed dealer. Simply cut out the coupon from your newspaper, and post it off with a cheque. If you sell the shares you buy through one of the licensed dealers who advertise in the press, you will be quoted a price without commision, and selling can be as easy as lifting the telephone.

Unfortunately, not all new issues are the same, and not all of them make life as simple for the would-be investor as they might. They come in four types: introductions; placings; offers for sale; and offers for sale by tender.

## Introductions

Introductions are no use to the stag. No new shares are on offer. All that happens is that jobbers start trading in shares which are spread around already. Usually, introductions involve a foreign company gaining a London listing. Sometimes they involve companies stepping up from the OTC market.

## Placings

Placings are nearly as bad. The sponsor (usually a stockbroker) fixes a price and the number of shares to be sold, and doles out three-quarters of them among his clients. The rest go to jobbers, who pass them on to brokers. This usually happens with companies coming to the USM. The boys in the know do a wonderful job for each other, and the outsider scarcely gets a look in.

## Offers for sale

What you really want is a straightforward offer for sale (see p.43 for offers for sale by tender). This will be arranged by the issuing house, usually a merchant bank or a broker. News of it will appear on most City pages in newspapers. Full details come in a prospectus, which has to be published in at least two national newspapers. Almost all of them appear in the *Financial Times*. They are also available direct from the issuing house.

A prospectus can run to 60 or 70 pages, and can be a daunting document. Plough through it, and you will end up with a headache and a hazy impression of what is going on. Do not be put off. The theory is that no one should buy shares in a new company without first being encouraged to read all about it. This theory is sound. In practice, however, the sheer bulk and complexity of a prospectus is enough to scare most people off shares for life. Do not worry. A prospectus is strictly an optional extra for anyone but the backroom boys.

*What you need to know*  All you need to know is what the City thinks about the shares. If the boys in the market do not fancy them, they do not have a chance, no matter what you think.

Finding out what they think can be as easy as asking your broker, reading the City pages (you will soon learn who gets it right most often) and watching what the licensed dealers are saying. None of them is infallible, but until you get pretty smart, they will do a lot better than you can on your own.

Your broker might frown at the thought, but you might find the licensed dealers the best guide of all. Check what price they are quoting before you post your cheque. However, be careful not to be tempted into trying to trade before you actually have any shares. You can only be sure of that when an allotment letter lands on your mat, officially certifying how many shares you have got.

Licensed dealers can trade in advance because they are effectively gambling on how the issue will go. They get a good idea by trading with some of the share-dealing syndicates who stag new issues on a giant scale, or with big institutions who are certain of getting shares because they act as underwriters and have so much cash in the game that they are bound to get something.

If any of your unofficial guides – brokers, press or licensed dealers – are uncertain, then opt out. Your chances of scoring as a stag will be slim. Only go ahead if you are convinced you have found a company you are ready to be with for a long stay. Then ask yourself what you know that the so-called experts have missed. And ask yourself if you want your head examining.

*Reading the prospectus*  A glance at the prospectus will tell you who is selling how many shares for how much. There will be pages about the past history and present state of the company, but only a little about its future. That is a shame, but the Stock Exchange imposes strict rules on profit forecasts to stop dubious promoters projecting an unrealistically rosy glow over what lies ahead. That makes sense.

There will be a profit record, perhaps a profit forecast, and a dividend forecast. And there will be a calculation of the price/

earnings ratio, and the dividend yield, two basic statistics to compare with other quoted companies in the same line of business. That gives an easy, worthwhile guide to roughly what the share price should be. Watch out. Do not be trapped into comparing the prospective – future – earnings ratio and dividend yield on the new issue with the historic – past – PE ratio and yield on other shares. It is easy to get a flattering idea of a new issue that way.

Deeper in the document will be words from the chairman on why the company is coming to market. The more cash being raised for expansion, the better. Find out whether the board are simply lining their own pockets. Feel more confident if the continuing directors are keeping a sizable stake, but not a majority of the shares. That way, they will be committed to working for themselves and the other shareholders, without the power to shoo away any would-be bidder without consulting shareholders. Check, too, how much pay is linked to profits. That helps. Share incentives are also good, though they should not be too generous. Around 5 per cent of the issued capital for directors, and another 5 per cent or so for employees, is reasonable. Frown at anything more.

*The names to watch* 'Who's who' is what matters next if the issue appeals to you. Check the sponsors – the merchant bank and the broker behind it. Even the City's finest make mistakes, or get greedy, and over-price issues. But the sponsorship of one of the better-known merchant banks or one of the livelier stockbrokers should mean that, at the least, the company is reasonably sound. The league table changes from time to time, so ask your broker about the current state of play. Sometimes someone hits a really hot streak – or goes stone cold.

In the first rank is almost any issue bearing the name of Barings, Morgan Grenfell, Kleinwort Benson, S. G. Warburg, Hill Samuel, Rothschild, Robert Fleming, Lazard Brothers, Schroder Wagg, Charterhouse, Samuel Montagu, Hambros, Barclays Merchant Bank, County Bank or Lloyds Merchant Bank. Firms such as Singer & Friedlander, Guinness Mahon and Brown Shipley are well up, and there are others who will do a perfectly satisfactory job. Be wary of the Americans until they have more of a record: their pricing may prove a trifle aggressive for our market.

Top of the broking heap is Cazenove, a firm of legendary placing power. If they push an issue, all of the boys will back it; they know they have to if they want to stay in the club. It is tempting to list other brokers, but the Big Bang has brought a transfer market in stockbroking stars. Today's winners could be working somewhere else tomorrow.

*Danger zone*   By now, you have probably got the message about the over-the-counter market: new issues abound there, but all should be treated with extreme caution. There are terrific winners, and total losers. Until you really know what you are doing, steer clear. Any company which has to resort to raising money this way is not good enough to qualify for the stock market proper. It may be a money-grabbing game, a short-term dash for cash or a new and untried venture. Reporting standards are variable, and the shares are sometimes promoted by pressure-selling methods. It is a market where beginners are regularly lured in by attractive half-promises, but only the wariest of gamblers should play.

*Form-filling tactics*   These are what count once you have decided to go for a new issue. A really successful launch can be oversubscribed 100 times, with £1000 million chasing £10 million worth of shares, so the odds are against you. Every application will be scaled down, and it is up to the issuing house as to how this is done. The bigger the demand, the smaller your chances of getting what you ask for – but the fatter the opening premiums will be when the dealings start on the stock market. What you lose on the swings, you may gain on the roundabout.

Some companies – such as British Telecom – deliberately favour small investors. This happens more often with the bigger, national names, who seek to buy a little goodwill by spreading their shares around. Smaller, more specialist operators may prefer fewer, larger shareholders, who will cost less to service. Watch the press for clues.

The more shares you ask for, the more you are likely to get. Many heavily subscribed issues hold a ballot to decide which of the smaller applications will get shares. The ballot may be weighted to favour the bigger applications, so while a cheque for £2000 may win no more shares than a lucky one for £200, the £2000 cheque may be ten times more likely to get something than the £200 cheque.

*Use your partner*   Your partner, husband or wife can be a vital investment aid. Never make one application where two will do – or perhaps three or four, adding in any children over the age of 18.

However, beware: since the British Telecom flotation, the game has changed. Instead of just being tossed out, multiple applications could lead to prosecution. The days are gone when your cat or your goldfish could make you a killing on the stock market. Now you must use the names of real people, with their permission. You can still assemble your own mini-syndicate of family and friends by making applications on their behalf, and paying them a small retainer or giving them a share of the profits.

Multiple applications, backed by a big bank overdraft, used to be a great game. Professional punters employed a small army of pensioners writing cheques, filling in application forms and addressing envelopes by the thousand. Even now, when the stags are running, City litterbins are stuffed with discarded prospectuses, each one with the application form torn out. Litter levels can be a useful clue to the likely success of an issue and so can newspaper sales counters: sometimes punters pull up with small vans to carry off hundreds of copies of the editions in which application forms are printed.

*Bullying the bank manager*  Bullying bank managers to extend sufficiently large overdrafts is also an important element in the stagging game. They know that you must put up more money than you will actually be required to pay in a big share issue. Normally, only cheques attached to successful applications are cashed, and because applications are scaled down, a cheque for part of that money is returned straight away. The loan is usually only needed for the few days before the shares can be sold and any outstanding cash repaid.

Officially, the banks are not too sure about stagging, but they can be cajoled and persuaded. Be they ever so exalted, bank managers are there to serve you. Ask for a stagging facility. If you earn enough, take out one of the gold credit cards, which entitle you to an automatic overdraft, or threaten to go elsewhere and get one if your bank manager hesitates.

*The application form*  Studying the application form pays off. It is no good asking for 1200 shares if the fine print says applications should be for units of 200 shares up to 1000 shares and in units of 500 shares thereafter. Anyone asking for 1200 will simply be disqualified. It is amazing how many bungle it.

Look carefully at the cut-off points. Try to pitch your application just above them. For example, where applications should be for units of 200 shares up to 1000 shares, then for units of 500 shares up to 5000 shares and finally for units of 1000 shares thereafter, it makes sense to go for 1500 shares, or for 6000 shares if you can raise the money. The sponsors have formed natural breaks at 1000 and 5000 shares, and may use them when scaling down.

Anyone applying for up to 1000 shares might get, say, 300; those asking for between 1000 and 5000 might get, say, 800; and people after more than 5000 might get 40 per cent of what they want. By going for a level just above the natural break, you might shift yourself up into a higher category of allotment. So, in the example, anyone asking for 6000 shares would get 2400, whereas applications for 5000 might get only 800. Sometimes that little extra on the application can pay off with a disproportionately large allotment.

And please, please, *please* pay attention to the closing date and time. Application lists almost always close at one minute past ten in the morning, usually only staying open longer if the issue is flagging. If you miss the post, or cannot reach the receiving bank on time, that is it. No sob stories, no amount of pleading, will get your application in. Miss the close, and you have had it.

*Traps for the unwary* All this may sound like marvellous fun, a magic way of making money, but there are traps for the unwary, the reckless and the feckless. Issues do flop. If you get it wrong and end up with more shares than you can afford, you might have to sell at a loss when dealings open. There is no way out. You cannot simply cancel your cheque if the issue looks like going bad. Once you have sent off your application, you are on the hook.

That explains the queues on the morning of an issue. Some people have too much cash riding on it to leave anything to chance. Post your application too far in advance and you run the risk of a last-minute change in the market mood. A promising issue could be left out in the cold, and your would-be winner could turn sour, after your cheque has gone in. The last-minute man in the queue has done all he can to avoid that happening.

*Offers for sale by tender*

Although all of these tactics for a straightforward offer for sale hold good for an offer for sale by tender, that has the added complication that the sponsors set a minimum price, and ask for offers at or above it. They want investors to do some of their work for them.

Once all of the applications are in, the sponsors set what is called the *striking price*, and all of the shares will be sold at that price. Anyone who bids at or above that price gets shares – at the striking price. If you are determined to buy, you can bid a silly high price. If everyone does the same, of course, everyone gets shares at a silly high price.

Sponsors choose to sell by tender when they are unsure what the price should be. This way they can judge the market mood, and set whatever price they wish, so long as there are enough bids at or above that price to sell all of the shares.

In practice, they will pitch the striking price below the maximum they could have got. They will leave some unsatisfied buyers who, they hope, will try to buy when trading starts, thus ensuring that the offer goes to a premium. But a big bonanza is unlikely. When it comes to judging how much you should tender, and whether you should play at all, your broker, the press and perhaps the licensed dealers will give the best guide. Good luck.

# 7  How to Pick a Share

Making a killing on the stock market must be easy, surely? Scan the back page of the *Financial Times*, and there is a list of major price changes. Frequently there are a dozen or more which have gone up by a healthy sum. It certainly cannot be too hard to pick a winner with so much on the move? Appearances, unfortunately, can be deceptive. We are all winners with the benefit of hindsight. Looking back, you knew what was going to happen. It is just that you did nothing about it at the time.

Doing it is different. When you actually have to lay out your own money, it gets much tougher. Suddenly you realize that there are 7000 securities to choose from. The dozen movers on the back of the *Financial Times* are very different to the two pages crammed with share prices inside.

Look more closely, and often there are nearly as many shares going down as there are going up. Some days, of course, almost all of them fall. Since January 1975, the UK market has been rising, but along the way there have been months and months when the mood was grim, when it was easy to lose a fortune – and lose it fast.

In 1985, for example, many caught a terrible cold in electronics. The darlings of 1984, they switched off a year later. The big boys were stuffed to the gills with STC, the former Standard Telephone & Cables company, when they slumped from 289p to 72p and began a desperate cutback programme. Acorn, the BBC computer star, all but went to the wall before Olivetti stepped in. And the receiver wound up Mettoy, the old Corgi toy group that had enjoyed a brief run on the strength of a personal computer which turned out to be not quite good enough.

Steady your nerves, though. Very few quoted companies actually go bust, and very few investors lose all of their money. Companies in trouble are nearly always rescued, and are often rebuilt into exciting new enterprises.

The arithmetic helps, too. If you lose half of your money, it sounds terrible, but your £1000 has only gone from £1000 to £500. Double it, and £1000 is £2000. On the down-side, you are out £500. On the up, you are £1000 better off. And in a rising market, the chances of doubling your money are much greater than the possibility of halving it.

## AN EXCUSE TO FALL IN LOVE

What you are looking for is an excuse to fall in love, a share to live and grow with. When Chancellor Nigel Lawson presented his Personal Equity Plan in the 1986 Budget, he said he wanted people to go directly into shares, choosing companies themselves, so that they would feel that the fortunes of their companies mattered to them. As political philosophy, and as an investment plan, it makes good sense.

It is a fine romance, picking the share to suit you. City pages parade the temptations before you. You might want to flirt with bid candidates or option market favourites, but whatever your fancy, check the fundamentals first. And that means examining the dividend yield and price/earnings ratio.

## THE DIVIDEND YIELD

This came up earlier as a simple reference point in weighing the worth of a new issue. Dividend yields form the bedrock of most measured investment decisions. It is no use picking the next takeover winner if the bid comes in below the market price (it happens sometimes) simply because gamblers got so carried away on the bid dream that they lost touch with investment reality, and wildly overvalued a company's shares.

The dividend yield will matter especially if income is high on your list of investment priorities. Capital gains are super, but dividends go on and on, year in, year out, no matter what the share price is doing. That can count a great deal for older shareholders, who may rely on such income. And, as we have seen earlier, a consistent and growing income stream is ultimately what many of the giant institutional investors are after.

Working out the dividend yield is not difficult. It is the percentage return from the annual income on a share. If you get £10 a year from an investment of £100, the yield is 10 per cent. If you buy 100 shares at £2 each, and get a dividend of 10p a share in the year, the dividend yield is 5 per cent. Calculate this by taking the total dividend received (10p multiplied by 100 shares equals £10), dividing this by the total

46

cost (£2 multiplied by 100 shares equals £200), and expressing it as a percentage – 5 per cent.

As the share price rises, the dividend yield falls, because you are paying more for the same amount of dividend. Conversely, the dividend yield rises when the share price falls, because you are buying the right to the same dividend more cheaply. If the dividend is increased, and the share price remains unchanged, the dividend yield rises. A higher dividend is likely to prompt a higher share price, and a reduced dividend, a lower one.

You do not normally have to work out yields yourself. They are shown in many newspaper share price tables, changing as prices change. Any broker will be able to tell you the yield on any share.

As a crude guide, the higher the yield, the more risky the share, and the more dubious the prospects. The lower the yield, the higher the company's growth rating. It all goes back to profit prospects, since profits ultimately determine how much dividend a company can pay.

The market is constantly revising its opinion, and this is reflected in changing share prices. Sometimes a good company with strong growth will offer a higher yield than others in the same business because few people have realized what is going on. That share will be worth buying. On the other hand, a high yield could mean that the City has spotted problems ahead. Profits may be on the slide, and the company may not be able to pay such a high dividend by the end of the year. Most published yields are based on the previous year's dividends, so they may overstate the true position, because the next dividend – the one you will actually get – could be cut, or they may understate the real yield if the company is doing well enough to raise the next dividend.

## PINNING YOUR FAITH ON THE PE

Pinning your faith on the price/earnings ratio, or PE, is one of the market's favourite games. Dividend yields have a certain down-to-earth reality about them: at the end of the day, you do get a dividend cheque through the post, and that means real money in your pocket. The PE means no such thing. It may just be a guess to build a dream on. PE is about mental, not physical jerks, and is the investment analyst's most powerful piece of ju-ju. (*see* p.16 for a full explanation of PE.)

Like the dividend yield, the PE is a key means of comparing one share with another. A high PE means that the market is normally

47

expecting fast profits growth. Or it may mean that a slump is expected this year, with last year's historic PE out on a limb as profits plunge – remember, most market rules can be turned on their head. A low PE usually means lower profits, or poor growth, are expected. Unless, that is, you know better, and have spotted a company with high growth and a low PE. Then you may have found a bargain. Take it to your heart.

## VARIATIONS ON THE THEME

There are, however, different strokes for different folks. The dividend yield or PE appropriate to one sector may not be right for another. Sometimes the market decides it has gone wrong, and a whole sector is re-rated, up or down. Sometimes the differences make sense. In 1986 it was hard to argue with lower price/earning ratios and higher dividend yields for oil stocks than for stores shares. That reflected the uncertain prospects for oil profits against the background of OPEC chaos, while strong consumer spending meant bright hopes for profits from High Street shops.

Much of it is fashion. It is easy to get sucked in, so try to keep your feet on the ground. City backroom boys do get it wrong, and get carried away by dreams of glory for different industries. We all ought to have known that the personal computer boom would go bust – and it did. Simple common sense should have suggested that the chance of fat profits would spring a flood of competitors, forcing everyone's margins down. But such common sense often eludes big investors as they run with the pack. Living in each other's pockets in the City, they are easily fooled when booming computer profits are the topic of conversation in every wine bar within half a mile of Throgmorton Street.

## WATCH THE AVERAGES

Keep a hold on reality by eyeing the averages. The best place to find them is in the *Financial Times*' 'Actuaries Share Indices'. A thumping great table full of them appears each day on the *FT*'s prices page. It splits the market into sub-groups, and gives average dividend yields and price/earnings ratios for each sub-sector, and for the market as a whole.

Obviously these continually shift with market moves, but if one sector gets far out of line, be extra cautious. You will need a very good case for investing in it. All too often, the sector which runs too far ahead is pulled back in line not by a roaring boom in profits, but by a slump – in industry profits or in share prices. Since the market always tends to overdo things – up or down – that could mean dramatic losses.

## PROSPECTIVE PROBLEMS

Be wary, too, of ambitious projections. In a rising market, those who once considered price/earnings ratios of 15 rather racy soon learn to feel comfortable with PEs in the 20s. Look hard. As the mood gets merrier, you may find they are not talking about historic PEs, based on last year's profits, but about prospective PEs – spurious sums based on guesses about this year's or next year's profits.

Any price/earnings ratio in excess of 20 needs a very special explanation, and should only be attached to a very special company indeed. Early in 1986, perfectly sane and respectable fund managers were beginning to cite prospective price/earnings ratios based on projected profits for 1990. They might have been right. They might have been mad. Either way, if they believed they were relying on anything other than pure guesswork, they were kidding themselves.

## ASSET BACKING – THE BACKSTOP

Once you are satisfied that the dividend yield and price/earnings ratio makes sense in the share of your choice, check the asset backing. This is the backstop. It gives you an idea of what the company might fetch if it stopped trading, the business was sold and the loans repaid.

Assets were described when the balance sheet was discussed (*see* p. 16). To discover the asset backing of a company, take the total value of assets – land, buildings, machinery, stocks, cash and such – deduct the liabilities – loans, tax due, creditors and so on – and you get Ordinary shareholders' funds. Divide this sum by the number of Ordinary shares in issue, and you have the asset backing per share. As usual, this is not something you have to calculate yourself. If you feel uncertain, ask your broker or dealer to check it for you.

Asset backing is not too important day-to-day. What matters is the profit earned from those assets. No one bothers much about the asset backing of Imperial Chemical Industries, where all eyes are on trading and no one seriously dreams of a takeover bid. However, assets can be very important if there is the chance of a bid. These days, there are precious few companies where you can rule this out completely, so it is always comforting to know that your company is sitting on a fat pile of assets. That can also be crucial when a company is in trouble, or is in one of two specialist categories – property companies and investment trusts (*see below*).

Obviously, the more assets the better, and the closer those assets are to cash the better. Look in the balance sheet for cash (minus overdrafts), or investments (saleable shares in other companies). There may also be a holding in an unquoted associate company, which may be in the books at nominal value but would perhaps be worth a great deal in a sale. Property comes next, the nearer London the better, and the older the date of valuation the better. Most companies list the date of the last valuation, or simply value their properties at what they cost originally. Any valuation more than two years old almost certainly means that the properties are worth more.

Plant and machinery is a more dubious plus. Though it is listed as an asset, much of it may be virtually worthless. Stocks (i.e. whatever the company manufactures etc.) are also uncertain: clearly, last season's fashions are worth little to a clothing company.

Ideally, you want a company which is trading well, and has an asset backing comfortably in excess of the share price. Then you are covered both ways – either the shares sell as a trading situation, or someone might take over the company and put the assets to better use to earn more profits.

Such companies are hard to find. The strongest asset situations crop up when a company has had a trading setback, and the price has fallen. Disappointing profits often leave assets looking cheap. You have to decide whether the setback is temporary, and whether those assets are worthwhile. That is not easy, but at least if you pick an asset-backed recovery company, the strength of those assets will help you sleep easier at night.

## PROPERTY COMPANIES AND INVESTMENT TRUSTS – ASSET EXCEPTIONS

Shares in property companies and investment trusts usually sell at a discount to assets (a price below the worth of what they own) as a matter of course. This discount ranges between 20 and 40 per cent, so you could find a company with 100p worth of assets whose shares sell at between 60p and 80p. Do not get carried away, thinking you have found a bargain. Almost certainly, the City will know about it: brokers have a sophisticated analysis service covering such things. Clearly there will be different views on the value of properties owned by different companies, especially where a large proportion of properties are actually being developed, but you will rarely catch the City out. The biggest property opportunities are usually in companies outside the property sector, when someone suddenly realizes that a factory would be worth much more torn down and the land used for offices.

Investment trusts are companies which hold shares in other companies. When the holdings are quoted shares – and many investment trusts have little else – the City can calculate the asset value precisely. Some trusts hold unlisted investments, and then there is room for debate over values, but surprises are rare. The size of the discount between the share price and asset value is determined by what the City thinks of the trust managers, and the chances of a bid.

Many trusts have been taken over or turned into unit trusts in recent years. Either way, shareholders can get out at close to asset value, and may have bought at a sizable (20 per cent plus) discount. Such brokers as Alexanders, Laing & Cruickshank. Wood Mackenzie or James Capel watch discounts closely, and keep lists of the big shareholders in each trust. Certain institutions are known to support bids for investment trusts – names such as London & Manchester, Save & Prosper, Cornhill. If they have a large slug of the shares, then the discount to asset value may be smaller than average because the trust is vulnerable to a takeover. (*See also* p. 60 for information on high-income shares.)

Investment trusts and property companies tend to be things apart, though investment trusts make an attractive alternative to unit trusts for the beginner. Their management charges are lower than those of unit trusts, dealing costs can also be lower, and the general trusts offer a good spread of risk. However, they do lack the thrills and spills of direct share dealing.

For the determined share punter, it is worth writing to the secretary of the bigger and brighter trusts, asking for a copy of the latest report and accounts. Simply looking at what these big, well-informed investors have bought and why provides useful investment ideas. Some names and addresses to contact are given at the end of the book.

## READING THE CITY PAGES

It is all very well arming yourself with the standard tools – the dividend yield, the price/earnings ratio and the asset value – but everyone can get them. What you must do before choosing the right share for you is to add your own touch, that something extra that will make you a share winner.

To do that you need to develop a feel for the market. Try to immerse yourself in it, so you can begin developing the trading instinct which will ultimately be your most valuable asset – except, perhaps, sheer good luck.

The simplest way to start is to scan the City pages regularly. Pay particular attention to the stock market report. The best is in the *Daily Mail*. The *Financial Times* market report concentrates on more predictable price movements. What you really want to know is what might happen next, not so much what has already happened.

### What makes prices move?

Prices move for a vast range of reasons. Companies announce profits and dividends, trading progress, orders, board changes or perhaps a bid approach. Rumours go round that any of those things may be about to happen, whether the company agrees or not. Directors visit stockbrokers for lunch and let things slip, or they brief big shareholders on progress (tricky this – remember, strictly speaking, all shareholders should have equal access to all information at the same time) or a party of brokers, institutional investors or journalists visits a factory. Perhaps a broker issues a circular, changing his profit forecast, or a newspaper or tip sheet makes a recommendation. The Government may announce retail sales figures, a spending squeeze, a tax change, new building plans. Interest rates may change, the pound rise, the price of oil fall. A director could buy a few shares, a big investor try to sell a large line. The option market may suddenly take off, and the price may be poised to penetrate an important point on a chartist's list (*see* pp. 88-90). And so on, and so on.

The list can be endless. Do not despair. No one knows everything. The price reflects all of these bits and pieces, jumbled together, misunderstood and manipulated by the investing community at large. When it comes to buying or selling, everyone gets the same share, no matter how much or little they know – or think they know.

### The City pages to watch

On the whole, the City pages are a good and fair guide, but obviously some are better-informed, with more intelligent judgements than others. The *Financial Times* carries the most weight. It covers almost every item of company and economic news, and frequently interprets it usefully. The 'Lex' column on the back page is required City reading, and may move share prices sharply.

The *Daily Mail* City page is widely accepted as a sharper, more readable companion to the *Financial Times*. It carries more gossip, more rumour, than the others, snatches of the kind of thing you might hear over lunch in the City. The 'Questor' column in the *Daily Telegraph* on a Monday offers sound share-tipping advice, and many of the heavy Sunday papers give share advice and gossip. Be wary, though, of investing on the strength of five- or six-line comments. These tend to be poorly researched, throw-away gossip, frequently planted by public relations advisers to the companies, or brokers with an interest in the shares. All too often, they are forgotten as soon as they appear, unless they hit lucky, and there is credit to be claimed later.

*Understanding the price tables*

The most comprehensive share price table is in the *Financial Times*, and interpreting it is something of an art. It has nine columns. The company's name is in Column 3, preceded by the highest and lowest share prices during the year. Next to the name comes the nominal value of the share (where that value is not 25p), and then the middle share price (*see* p. 29). For example, in the market, the price may be 70p to 74p, so the middle price in the *Financial Times* will be 72p.

The next column carries the change in the middle price on the day. Then comes the amount of dividend last declared, or officially forecast by the company. The next figure is the *cover* – the number of times that profits available for a dividend would cover such a payment (e.g. a figure '2' means the company's distributable profits are twice the sum required to pay that dividend – the higher the cover, the safer the dividend). The next column shows the gross dividend yield (before deduction of tax), and the final column gives the price/earnings ratio based on profits in the company's last report and accounts. On a Monday, the high and low columns (i.e. columns 1 and 2) are replaced by the columns giving the months in which the interim and final dividends are normally paid – useful for investors who need to plan their flow of income.

Many investors only buy the *Financial Times* on a Saturday, when the two prices pages are supplemented on an inside page by a list of actual Stock Exchange deals, across the board. This simply carries company names, with prices – nothing else. It is useful because it records trades in obscure stocks not covered elsewhere in the press. These are taken from the Stock Exchange Official List, which is published daily. Copies of that, with prices of all shares traded in London, can be found in main libraries.

Other newspapers' share price lists follow a pattern similar to the *Financial Times*, however without so many columns or so much information.

### Market capitalization

The *Financial Times* has many of the most crucial things you need to know about a share, all on one line. However, the asset value is absent, and so, too, is one useful figure which appears in the prices table in *The Times* on Mondays. This gives the stock market capitalization of the company – the value of the company as determined by multiplying the number of shares in issue by the share price. This can be invaluable. Whenever anyone enthuses to you about a company, ask the market capitalization. It gives you a quick check on whether you are talking about a tiddler, or a company of substance, putting the gossip into perspective in a flash. It is amazing how often enthusiasm comes crashing to earth when you learn that some would-be winner is already valued at many millions more than you might expect. It also provides a quick check on the plausibility of bid rumours. Smaller companies are starting to make cheeky bids for bigger brothers, but normally the would-be bidder needs to be at least as large as its target.

### All the exes

Any price table bears cryptic *ex*es every so often: *ex* dividend, *ex* scrip, *ex* rights. The *ex* means 'without'. If you buy a share ex dividend (or 'xd'), it means you will not have the right to a recent dividend attached to the shares. Ex scrip (or 'ex cap', or 'xc') means you buy without the right to a recent scrip issue. And ex rights (or 'xr') means the shares no longer have the right to a recent rights issue.

Sometimes share prices may seem to fall sharply. Look closely, and you will find that they have gone ex scrip, or ex rights, and that is what has done it. For example, shares which are ex a one-for-one scrip issue will halve in price because there will be twice as many of them from that point. The opposite to *ex* is *cum* (meaning 'with') which means you buy with the rights to a dividend, scrip or rights issue.

### Issues, highs and lows, and options

The stock market report page of the *Financial Times* also carries the prices of recent issues, both from newly floated companies and from established ones. There is a list of the most active stocks on the previous day, and of share highs and lows in the previous session. These are worth studying. Prices do not move without a reason. Sometimes that reason will be widely known, but if it is not, try to find out what is going on. Somebody, somewhere, thinks they know something, good or bad.

Similar remarks apply to the list of traditional option business. I will look at options in more detail later (*see* pp. 108-14), but if someone has bought a *call option* in a particular share, by and large they are expecting something good. A *put option* suggests bad news, and a *double option* means action, impact uncertain. In practice, the messages are not as simple as that, but watching the option list is a useful way of keeping on the alert.

## INVESTMENT MAGAZINES

The two main investment magazines are the *Investors Chronicle* and the *Financial Weekly*. Any half-serious investor ought regularly to read the *Investors Chronicle* which is stuffed with valuable advice. Unsung, but immensely worthwhile, is the back section which analyses all company results and reports and accounts. This provides the basic statistics, plus the handiest calculation of asset values.

*Financial Weekly* is much less sophisticated, but carries a useful table of over-the-counter market share prices, although these will be several days out of date. It also devotes a couple of pages to summaries of stockbrokers' circulars on various companies. Again, these are usually way out of date, but give a glimpse of what the professionals are looking at – and which broker to approach to try and beg a copy.

*What Investment?* is lively, with an erratic mixture of tips and advice on family finance. *Money Magazine* is paying increasing attention to shares, with a solid family finance base.

## TIP SHEETS

Tip sheets – investment newsletters – can be worthwhile. The most prominent is the *Fleet Street Letter*, and deservedly so. It is quite racy, but backed by solid research and a lot of good sense. The *IC Newsletter* is linked to the *Investors Chronicle*: it has a patchy record, and is poorly presented.

If you want an alternative view, Bob Beckman produces a couple of newsletters boasting ferocious, highly detailed research. The *Investors Bulletin* is more general but, for many years now, has been preaching an aggressively apocalyptic view of share prices and the Western economies.

Other tip sheets should be approached with more caution. Some have a reputation for allowing their ideas to leak, and the prices of their tips go up before the recommendations reach subscribers, even though all claim to take precautions. In any event, tip sheet recommendations tend to be marked up by the jobbers on the morning the tip sheet appears, so readers may find it difficult to buy at the recommended prices, especially as others may be scrambling to do the same. Other newsletters are less ready to advise on selling tips than they might be. None the less, do not write them off completely. A good tip sheet is worth taking, especially in a rising market.

## OTHER SOURCES OF INFORMATION

Where else can you go for company clues? Your local library, for a start. Check their reference works, and stock of newspapers and magazines – you might find some surprisingly useful things. If, for example, the love of your life should suddenly become a company in the fruit trade, some libraries may stock the *Fruit Trades Journal* or whatever. Pop in once a month to scan the file, and you might pick up valuable tips about the fruit business and, perhaps, advance news of your company. Trade papers often beat the nationals to the punch on their specialized subjects, and now and then, they could put you on the path to something big before the investment world realizes what is happening. The bigger the library, of course, the better your chance of finding useful publications.

Major libraries should also stock Extel cards. These are produced by Exchange Telegraph, and are the standard reference sources for stockbrokers, newspapers and major investors. There is an Extel card for every quoted company, and cards covering the unlisted securities market, the over-the-counter market, larger private companies and foreign companies.

The cards may appear complicated, but will repay a little study. They tell you what the company does, its address, the names of its registrars (who keep records of all shareholdings), plus a detailed version of profits stretching back several years. They also show who owns 5 per cent (or more) of the shares, how the price has moved over the years, what the balance sheet looks like, the net asset value, details of dividends, and a potted version of recent announcements. The cards are constantly updated.

Extel cards are a number-cruncher's delight – though do not get too carried away with them. Remember, they contain a record of the past, and when you buy a share, you are looking to the future.

Libraries may also carry the *Stock Exchange Weekly Official Intelligence*. It lists all share prices, plus dealings by directors – very useful. The *Stock Exchange Official Yearbook* may also be there. That has basic information about a company's capital and recent profits but runs very much a second-best to the Extel cards.

If you work in the City, there is a specialized business library which is worth a lunch-time visit. The librarians are very helpful, and there is an enormous range of specialist publications.

Then there are the companies themselves. Never hesitate to write to any which appeal to you. Check the registered address on an Extel card or in the Stock Exchange Yearbook and write to the company secretary, asking for the latest report and accounts, and anything else they have to offer. Almost invariably, you will get a helpful reply.

Watch too, for newspaper advertisements from companies, reporting their progress. And pay special attention to unit trust advertisements: sometimes they list shares the trusts hold – a share tip of sorts.

Write to the more successful unit trust managers (there are regular progress reports and league tables in the City pages on Saturday and Sunday). They will send you their reports, listing which shares they hold, and what they have been buying and selling. Top investment trusts are similar. They will send their annual report, with tables showing what they hold – super stuff.

With a little application, you can pick the brains of all manner of investment experts for the price of a postage stamp. An inventive investor need never feel alone out there. There is always a queue of professionals waiting to impress you. Just keep reminding yourself that they get it wrong sometimes, too.

# 8 Share Personalities

The deeper you delve into the market, the more you find that shares are not simply boring bits of paper. They come alive. Companies and their shares have very distinct personalities. Some you will like, others you will loathe. Consciously or not, you will find yourself drawn to certain types. Try to step back and rationalize it rather than letting it sneak up on you. Otherwise, one morning you might wake with a start, and realize you have a share portfolio which is extremely unsuitable for what you are trying to achieve.

## BUILDING A PORTFOLIO

Conventional wisdom will tell you to spread your investments to reduce your risk. No share can be absolutely safe, and the most unexpected things can, and do, happen. If you hold, say, ten different shares, the chances of all of them going wrong are modest, unless the whole market collapses. You can afford a shock or two if the other eight or nine companies are in good health. Within that ten, you ought to have a mix of industries – not all stores or oil shares, for instance. And while you might be able to afford the odd, small, speculative company, it is best to balance it with a solid chunk of major names, which are less likely to produce nasty surprises.

That sort of advice would win a nod of approval from most investment advisers: build a portfolio with a sensible profile. And yet . . . you may not have enough cash to spread your risks too widely. The investor with £2000 can have great fun, but would look daft with £200 each in ten companies. Dealing costs alone would eat a great chunk of cash.

Even if you have cash enough to spread wider – say, £1000 each in ten shares – that may not suit your temperament. Picking one good share is tough enough, let alone ten. And one or two winners, even if they doubled, might still not give the game enough sex appeal.

Perhaps you are ready to take a greater gamble, with an altogether riskier portfolio. If you really are using money you can afford to lose – and that is the way you should view your first foray into the stock market – you might be more inclined to split your £2000 between just two companies, or even £10,000 between three or four, in the hope of a worthwhile killing if you can spot a winner or two. Do it, if that is how you feel.

Do not allow the experts to dictate to you. Many people are prepared for a gamble, and are less concerned about doing things the risk-averse, responsible way.

Certainly, for many who are tempted into the stock market by the Chancellor's Personal Equity Plan, the sense of splitting £200 a month, or £2400 a year, between too many shares is questionable. But for those who do, the most popular City line will be to shuffle the cash into blue chips, shares with a safe, middle-of-the-road personality.

## BLUE CHIPS

Blue chips are the cream of the crop, shares in the biggest, best and safest companies, such as Marks & Spencer, National Westminster Bank, Prudential Assurance, Imperial Chemical Industries, Boots and Hanson Trust. These days, blue chip companies are likely to be valued at £1000 million or more, and will be firms most people know a little about.

All of the 30 companies whose shares make up the Financial Times Ordinary share index qualify as blue chips. It is possible to deal in large quantities of them at a time – say, 50,000 or more – with a narrow spread between buying and selling prices. That makes trading them relatively cheap. Because they are so well-established, they are widely assumed to be safe investments.

It ain't necessarily so, though. They got their name from the highest-valued chips in a poker game, and they can be quite a gamble. The price of Thorn EMI, for example, swung between 300p and 492p in 1985. Imperial Chemical Industries moved between 630p and £10, and Barclays Bank between 333p and 590p. Terrific stuff when they are going up, but tough when they are falling.

By and large, however, blue chips are safer than the average share, and less likely to spring nasty surprises. They are well researched by the big City investment houses and, though the increasing US involvement in our leading shares can bring sharp price changes, tend to move in nice, steady lines, giving the investor ample time to think carefully and move in or out without pressure to act in undue haste. No one will suggest you have made a bad mistake buying a blue chip, and you should sleep safe at night with them.

## HIGH-INCOME SHARES

This book is slanted towards the seeker after capital growth, rather than the investor who wants high income. Fixed-interest investments offer the highest income, but lack the capital gains potential to resist the steady drip of inflation, which gradually erodes the value of capital. However, high-income shares combine a good return with the chance of some capital gain. Spotting them is relatively easy, though picking a winner is tougher. Look down the list of dividend yields, decide what return you want and place strong emphasis on the dividend cover. The higher the cover, the further profits can fall before a company is forced to cut the dividend. Safety counts a lot with income stocks.

Unfortunately, you will find that the highest high-income shares are the riskiest ones. The yield may be high because it might not be there tomorrow. In 1986, the highest yields were in gold and oil shares. The dangers were obvious.

It is always worth looking, though, at investment trusts for high yield. Where you see a trust with two or three classes of shares, you will find high-yielding income shares. These come with split-level trusts, clever little schemers which credit most of the capital growth they earn to the capital shares, and almost all of the income to income shares. Be warned, though: there are often special conditions attached to such shares, and you should only buy after taking advice from a broker who specializes in investment trusts – the likes of Laing & Cruickshank, Wood Mackenzie or James Capel.

Shrewdly selected high-income shares can outperform a growth portfolio, especially when the actual income is taken into account. On total return, high-yield unit trusts frequently come near the top of the charts. In an uncertain market, shares with a high yield are presented as having defensive qualities, the notion being that their greater dividend return will save them from falling as far as shares which have only a tiny yield. Thus, when the going gets tough, investors concentrate on dividend yields as a much surer thing than capital growth.

It sounds plausible, and has some truth. In practice, however, the income prop may prove modest. When the whole market is falling, the good go down with the bad. Higher-yielding shares fall with the rest, and the market looks for higher yields from everything. High-income shares may not fall as far as out-of-favour growth stocks (*see below*), but fall they will. It is little consolation that you may be losing less than the next chap. You are still losing money, and that is not the idea of investment.

Where high-income shares do well, they do it for the classic reason – the higher the risk, the higher the return. If they come right, the capital gain is greater. So when you opt for a high-income buy – outside fixed-interest shares – you may be taking on a riskier proposition than you realize. Do it with your eyes open. Unless you know better – and are sure of it – higher return really does mean higher risk.

## GROWTH STOCKS

Growth stocks are heavenly, the investment everyone dreams about, shares that go on and up supported by a busy board and ever-expanding profits. You never intend, of course, to buy anything but growth stocks. After all, you are not laying your money down to see it sit and do nothing.

In stock market terms, the growth stock commands a higher price/earnings ratio than average, and a lower dividend yield. The idea is that you accept lower returns today for growth tomorrow. Such stocks need to be in fashionable industries, run by fashionably alert directors, ready to expand by organic growth and by acquisition.

Growth stocks are not always what they seem. Great Universal Stores, for example, has long been the slumbering High Street and mail order giant. It hardly ranks as a fashionable growth stock, yet it has a 35-year record of unbroken growth. Beauty, though, is in the eye of the beholder, and not too many trendy eyes have glanced the way of GUS through the years.

Expansion by acquisition is one of the key elements in the growth stock game. It can mean frequent issues of highly rated shares, perhaps supplemented by increased borrowings to mix a little cash in any takeover bait.

The idea is that a company with shares boasting a price/earnings ratio of 20 can gobble up a company on a PE of 10, and gain a fresh injection of growth. If both companies are the same size a price/earnings ratio of 20 merged with one of 10 will produce a company with a price/earnings ratio of 15. Mix in the notion that the two together can save costs, apply the talents of growth stock management to the lowly-rated acquisition, and suddenly the City can be

61

persuaded that a price/earnings ratio of 15 is too modest for this exciting new animal. It should really sell on a PE of, what? Shall we say 20? So the shares rise, and the game can start again after a pause for digestion. It is wonderful how figures on the back of an envelope can start a minor industrial revolution, rationalizing British industry and all of that – with a profit or two for the bankers, brokers and share punters along the way.

Using highly valued shares to bid is a splendid way of buying other companies and their profits on the cheap. Bid for them with cash, and it could cost perhaps 15 per cent in interest charges on that cash. Bid using high-flying shares, and the effective cost could be as low as the dividend yield on those shares – perhaps 2 per cent. Once issued, though, shares are for ever. Dividends have to be paid on them, and profits earned for them, year in, year out. Bank borrowings can always be repaid to cut interest costs.

The pluses and minuses are complex, but when a share is running, few pause to argue. For budding entrepreneurs building growth companies, the main problem can be ensuring that they do not issue too many shares, leaving themselves too small a slice of the cake.

Growth stocks are great when the market is rising. The growth in profits keeps coming through, and the constant flow of deals makes it difficult to be too critical about what is organic, sustainable growth, and what is a one-off killing along the way, helped by merger accounting tricks. Growth stocks can even be forgiven one hiccup in the profit record, provided the reasons seem sensible. Two hiccups, though, can be fatal to the share rating, and the game stops.

Always remember: few stocks grow for ever. The bigger they get, the tougher it is to keep up the pace, the bigger the deals needed. Always stand by the door, ready to leave with a profit should you start to grow uneasy.

## RECOVERY STOCKS

Recovery stocks are simply super – provided they actually recover. You find them in industries which have fallen from favour – metal bashers and electronics have been classic hunting grounds in recent years – or among businesses which have hit the odd, unhappy year or two. Unfortunately, it is easy to wade into a depressed company which is going to stay that way, or go on down.

Look for signs of firm management. Tough though it may be on the workers involved, factory closures and redundancies can be good news to the investor, along with sales of subsidiary companies. Swift surgery can work wonders in reviving profits. Talk of British industry emerging leaner and fitter from the hard times of the early 1980s was right. Lower overheads leave more profits.

Companies which have been cutting back often find a bonus in the pension fund. Watch for companies where there has been a heavy reduction in staff. There may be scope for lower contributions to the pension fund, boosting profits.

Management changes are important. Perhaps the most successful boardroom revolution in recent years was at the Rank Organisation, sparked by the Prudential Assurance and other big investors. They ousted the old board, and put in Sir Patrick Meaney as chairman and Michael Gifford as managing director. They cut sharply and swiftly, and transformed Rank.

Such management coups happen frequently, some quietly, some with a great fuss. Watch for board changes, and stories of big compensation payments. That means someone has been given the boot in favour of new managers who the big shareholders believe can do better.

Changes at the top often pep the share price. They make a good each-way bet. Either the new team rebuilds the business, or a bidder steps in. The changes swing the spotlight on to the company, and the new managers find themselves working under threat of a takeover should they fail to make a good impression. After a few months in the hot seat, they almost invariably trot around to the major City investors, keen to say what a good job they can do, begging them not to become impatient and encourage would-be bidders. That, too, helps the share price.

Always, though, pay special attention to the assets of any recovery stock. If there is no recovery, the assets will matter if the company goes bust. And it is the assets which will allow a new management to build a better company, or will attract a bidder. Avoid companies with heavy borrowings, unless there are parts which can quickly be sold to cut debt.

## PENNY STOCKS

Once upon a time, penny stocks were what the name suggests – shares that sold for a few pence. Now anything under £1.00 is liable to be called a penny stock, and a whole industry has grown up around them, with unit trusts and tip sheets.

They are appealing because they appear to give you more for your money. Buying 5000 shares for 10p each seems better than spending the same £500 on 100 shares at £5.00 each. However, there are snags. The dealing spread – the gap between what you buy for and what you sell for – is fatter, and works against you. Shares with a middle price of £5.00 might well be 495p to sell, 505p to buy – a spread of 10p, or 2 per cent. The 10p shares will probably be 9p to sell, 11p to buy – a spread of 2p, or 20 per cent. Your penny share has to work much harder before you clear the dealing costs.

When a penny share moves, it moves faster than a heavier-priced share because it takes proportionately bigger steps. On a 10p share, the next price up will be 10½p, a theoretical 5 per cent gain (though you are still a long way from making money). The £5.00 share may have moved to 505p, a gain of 1 per cent. When a share is sliding, a penny stock seems to race away from you. A fall from 10p to 9½p means that shares which may have cost 11p will only fetch 8½p to sell – a hefty loss with what might be the first change in price.

All the while, the investment fundamentals remain the same for a penny stock as for a heavyweight. A share selling at 10p is theoretically worth the same as one selling at £5.00 if they are both on a price/earnings ratio of 20, and a dividend yield of 2 per cent.

The lesson comes home clearly when there is a scrip issue or a share split. If our share trading at £5.00 had a nominal value of £1.00, and the board decided to split each £1.00 nominal share into ten shares of 10p nominal value, the price would fall to 50p for each share – but since there would be ten of them for every one held previously, there would be no change in the real value of the company.

There is some merit in the argument that penny shares have more room to grow than the big boys. ICI is unlikely to grow ten-fold over the next decade, whereas a low-priced stock just might. But it might not. Penny-share fans are really saying that they have found a gambling stock which might take off, and are backing that instead of some big, established company in a more mature stage of development, with less risk. The old maxim of high risk, high reward creeps back in.

That is not to knock penny stocks – they can be terrific fun – but many of them are in small, highly speculative companies. Just be sure you realize that.

Their main attraction, in the end, comes back to the psychological factor – they simply feel cheaper. Laughable in theory, this is important in practice. Tip sheets and licensed dealers are always keen to follow low-priced shares. They know they will find more takers for them than for the heavyweights. And the more takers, the more the price will rise.

# 9    The Shell Game

Company directors are only human. They are in the great stock market game for much the same reasons as you are – the fun and the money. They only begin to tune in to the notion of a knighthood, building a business for posterity, the good of the nation and all that other ego-boosting stuff in their later years. Having fun and making money amount to very nearly the same thing for most company directors. So long as they are making the money for their company and building a rising share price, then the interests of directors and investors coincide nicely. That is the angle to watch – the way the money goes.

Making money retains a fascination for company promoters long after it would seem to satisfy the wildest dreams of most people. The first million matters because that is oney to live on. The next however many tens of millions matter, too, because by then the promoters have been trapped by the game. Every extra penny is another point gained. The money itself may not matter, but the score certainly does. And if you have built up a thriving public company, then you are concerned about playing the game.

Brilliant money-making players pop up every so often at the head of a new issue, and we have already explored how to get a piece of the new-issue action. Just as often, though, the real movers try their hand at the shell game. And spotting candidates for the shell game can be one of the most rewarding of all stock market moves.

Shells come in all shapes and sizes, generally the smaller the better. The idea is to take control of a company which is no longer going anywhere much, pop an unquoted business into it and use this as the base on which to build. The companies going in will generally be too small or too young to gain a quotation in their own right. Put a group of them together under bright management, and you can build an exciting business fast – and highly profitably.

## THE FIRST CLUES

The would-be shell promoter will want a company where he or she can buy control, or at best a 29.9 per cent stake, as cheaply as possible. Profits may not matter, but ideally the target company will have some assets, preferably cash, or assets which can be turned into cash fairly easily – properties, share stakes or perhaps one or two subsidiaries which the outgoing management might buy. Often the shell will have hit a poor patch of trading under long-established directors nearing retirement, who lack the heart for the major reshaping the business may need.

The new promoter may start by quietly building a small share stake, only going up to 4.9 per cent and sitting just short of the 5 per cent at which he has to announce his presence. He may then try to get the board to sell him more shares. Watch for announcements of share stakes. Everyone keeps an eye open for them, and sometimes prices soar as soon as a new 5 per cent plus investor pops up. However, there is a risk in leaping in after a big rise: the new would-be hero may be blocked by the board, or unable to buy more shares because the price has run away from him; in some cases, he may simply be an investor, making his presence public in the hope that the price will leap, and allow him to get out with a quick profit. Sometimes the lack of any sizable price move can be disturbing. It may mean that the market men know that nothing is going to happen, or it may just mean you have spotted one they have missed. Try to make doubly sure. Usually, however, the patient investor will come to no harm by following what the professionals do.

The first real move comes when the new promoter moves in publicly. This will involve either buying shares from the board and making a full bid for the rest, or selling a company to the larger one for enough shares to give him control – either option is promising. A full cash bid will usually be way below the share price, and holders will not be expected to take it. Such a bid has to be made by anyone taking more than 29.9 per cent of a company. If it comes, check who is underwriting it – that is, providing the cash. That will give a clue to the muscle behind the new promoter.

If he is selling a company in, check who the professional advisers are – the bankers, the stockbrokers and the auditors. The bigger the names, the better. Check, too, if they are staying on as advisers to the company. The right names will be more acceptable to the City for future deals, and it is important to get them involved as early as possible.

# READING THE PLANS

Watch, too, for the type of company that is going in, and what the new boss has to say of his plans. At this stage, it does not matter too much what they are, so long as they indicate firmly that expansion by acquisition is on the menu. Organic growth (i.e. growth from within a company) is fine for established operators, but newcomers need to buy their way to growth as well. Stock Exchange rules sometimes make it tricky to signal the ultimate direction. Companies are supposed to stay in roughly the same line of business, and any radical change may need to be made by stages; any really big deal must be approached slowly. Minnows are not allowed to swallow whales without a mass of red tape, so small fish have to be fattened carefully before the big bite, for fear of frightening the authorities.

No matter how implausible the official expansion story, the mere appearance of someone new will be enough to generate excitement. Players rarely get beyond Stage 1 without lining up well-informed support. It may not be equal treatment for all, but insiders have their uses – and the money to back promising newcomers with big ideas.

What you want is a hungry newcomer, keen to make his fortune by buying businesses. Unfortunately, hungry newcomers are not allowed to advertise their intentions too openly in the documents they send to shareholders, but they can give a few clues.

## SPOTTING THE HUNGRY YOUNG MEN

Look hard at any potted career history in the documents, and note the age of the new chief executive. Anyone under the age of 28 is suspect; so is anyone over 52. Ideally, you want someone with a measure of experience, and time, ambition and energy enough to build something big – a hungry young man. If he has worked with major companies, see how he can apply his experience in the shell.

Most important of all, see how he takes his share stake. Watch what price he has paid, either by buying shares or the value put on shares he is taking in exchange for any company he is selling in. Check, too, if there are restrictions on when he can sell them, and if he has options to take more shares, perhaps linked to profit targets. Check what price he will pay, and when he will get his extra shares. Comb the fine print at the back of the document, looking through the material contracts to see if he has done other deals for shares. Work out the price he has paid. And scan his contract of employment, to see whether he earns a slice of profits. The deeper he is committed, the harder he will work.

Watch, too, for share deals among his supporters and advisers. Perhaps his brokers are underwriting shares, and placing them with clients. Perhaps some institution is taking shares for the first time, or has agreed to stay on for the ride. Any sign of support from big money, smart money, is good.

And, of course, you should watch the financial press for clues, interviews with the new man and so on.

## DANGER SIGNALS

In a rising market, the honeymoon will normally last for about six months or until the first sizable deal – whichever comes first. If nothing has happened after six months, beware. Something is wrong. Sell, unless you can establish very good reasons for staying on.

Now and then, a promising shell is used to float smallish companies dominated by family directors with little experience outside their own business. Tread carefully. This kind of deal sets the family up nicely, and rakes in fat fees for the original finders of the shell and for those who got in before the action started. However, there may be no great follow-through, as the family sit with the prestige of a public company, selling shares from time to time and watching their business grow, with no dynamic plans for expansion.

## RECONSTRUCTIONS

Managed carefully, a successful shell can be built into a stock market monster. Profits from picking the right one and sticking with it can be enormous. Polly Peck was just such a shell company: when Turkish-Cypriot economics graduate Asil Nadir moved in, the price was 9p; it hit £36 within three years. Polly may be the most spectacular example, but in recent years, there have been dozens of other shells that have turned into stock market rockets.

The purists, perhaps, might argue over definitions. Some of the big winners might be called reconstructions, rather than shells. But the principles are the same: spot a modest company which is not going anywhere, reshape it and pump in new businesses to generate growth. The reconstruction may be a little more difficult to spot, because the chosen company may not look such an obvious case for treatment, and the first deal or two may not be particularly large. But they are well worth hunting out.

## FUND-RAISING

Definitions do not matter. What you want is the action, in a shell or a reconstruction. Either way, if you miss the first stage, you may be able to join in when the first real fund-raising exercise is launched. Most new boys with big ideas will want more cash pretty quickly; it will make life easier for them in a myriad of ways. The most popular method is by a rights issue – offering new shares to existing investors at a special price.

This expands the company's capital base, widening the scope for bank and other borrowings. It also allows the promoter, or his backers, to raise their stake cheaply. The price of the rights will usually be pitched well below the market price, but well above the real worth of the company. It is a classic way of using the market, translating hope into hard cash, which can then be employed – if all goes well – to justify that hope, and generate a still greater premium for even more hope.

The fund-raising usually sends the price up at first. Then it might sit quietly for a spell while the market waits for the next move. That is the time to buy. If you have got in earlier, always take up your rights issue if you can. Fund-raising is one of the surest signs that action is in the offing.

## WHAT YOU WANT TO SEE

Once aboard, stay in for the ride so long as it feels good. What you want to see are:

● an increase in earnings per share with each deal.

● signs that each deal brings in cash, either in the company being bought through selling assets or through fund-raising.

● rising dividends.

● directors raising their share stake by options or by further purchases.

● a price/earnings ratio which stays above the average.

● a stable core of top managers.

● a stable set of top City advisers.

● the emergence of sizable shareholders among big City investors.

● at least one significant deal every nine months.

## WHAT YOU DO NOT WANT

Investment fashions change, the economy may slump or your super-star promoter could stumble, so watch for danger signs. The things you do not want are almost a mirror image of the good signs listed above. You do not want:

● deals which cut earnings per share.

● increasing debt.

● large share sales by the board.

● static dividends.

● a price/earnings ratio down to single figures.

● constant management changes.

● changes in City advisers.

● long periods without expansion news.

● the top man joining other companies and/or taking a seat on government bodies, the CBI or City authorities.

● directors telling the press the shares are cheap.

● a move to new headquarters in Mayfair.

● talk of moving into financial services.

Tread carefully, too, once the market capitalization exceeds £500 million: by that stage, it may be more difficult to find suitable things to buy. Tread even more carefully when the capitalization goes over £1000 million: the company may still prosper, but the shares are less likely to double or treble in a year. They may still do nicely, but the earlier excitement may have faded. Stay with them, but take some profits. This may no longer be the go-go stock you bought.

## F. H. TOMKINS: A TEXTBOOK SHELL

The rise and rise of F. H. Tomkins under Greg Hutchings is a textbook example of how to take a sleepy company and build it into a high flyer.

Hutchings gained a degree in engineering at Aston University, worked as an engineering consultant and researcher for a City fund manager, and spent three years as corporate development manager at Hanson Trust.

In 1983, backed by County Bank and stockbrokers Simon & Coates, he borrowed enough to buy 24 per cent of Tomkins, a sleepy Midlands nuts-and-bolts business making pre-tax profits of under £1.5 million, and valued at under £8.5 million. He set about increasing efficiency and brought in tighter financial controls and staff incentives – and in the process impressed sufficient investors to win Tomkins shares an above-average price/earnings ratio.

Early in 1984, he bought a distributor of specialist motor components for £2.2 million in cash. In January 1985, he bid £4 million for Hayters, a lawnmower manufacturer, financing the deal by issuing convertible loan stock. In August 1985, he bought six companies from GKN for £10.7 million.

By April 1986, he was confident enough to bid £170 million for tap and valve maker Pegler-Hattersley. At that point, Tomkins had a stock market value of £120 million. Tomkins forecast that profits would double to £7.1 million for the year to May 1986, and earnings and dividends continued to rise. When the Pegler bid went in, Tomkins shares were on a prospective price/earnings ratio of 27, and a historic 43. The Pegler PE was 14, the industrial average.

The astronomic Tomkins share rating allowed Hutchings to use high-flying paper to go for Pegler, a company making pre-tax profits of £18 million, with vastly bigger assets than Tomkins and with a reputation for sleepy management. The belief that he would be able to squeeze more profit out of Pegler made the bid possible, and Hutchings made it clear that he intended to go on to bigger and bigger companies.

When he bought in to Tomkins, its shares were 30p; in three years, with the Pegler bid, they were 325p. Hutchings had by now made his first million or two, after repaying what he had borrowed to buy into Tomkins – and had money-making options on more Tomkins shares.

# 10  The Bid Bonanza

Gone are the days when a takeover bid was a big event. Nowadays they are commonplace, and no company can consider itself safe. Some of the most famous names in British industry have tumbled – tobacco giant Imperial Group, Scotch whisky aristocrats Distillers and High Street chains such as Currys, Debenhams and British Home Stores. Rumours swirl around almost any company you can think of, and even a stock market valuation of £4000 million is not enough to ensure immunity.

If you are a share trader, forget the debate about whether or not bids are good for Britain, good for industry or serve the consumer well. What matters is the chance of quick, fat profits. A bid is the great bonus, a short-cut to capital gains which might have taken years to come by profits growth alone. Never mind the industrial strategy; enjoy the thrill of a soaring share price.

Some of the most beautiful shares on the stock market are growing companies which have bid prospects thrown in. Choose carefully, and you have a triple winner: a share which rises because trading is good and profits are rising; a share which bobs higher on rumours of a bid; and – O happy day! – a share which leaps when a bid actually appears.

## SPOTTING A BID STOCK

Finding such a stock can be hard, but not impossible. There are clues a'plenty. Unfortunately, there are no guarantees. Some stocks remain bid stocks for a full 20 years or more, always the bridesmaid and never the bride. It would be tempting fate to mention them here. There are believers clinging to every one, convinced that the offer will have arrived by the time you read this.

The ideal bid stock will have a good profits record, heavy asset backing, a fair spread of investors without large blocks of shares stuck with a small number of long-term holders (or large blocks with known predators), and a slice of a growing section of industry. That is pretty near the ideal stock, let alone the ideal bid stock. Find any two of those qualities, and you will be in with a fair chance.

### Profit margins

Look, too, for established names which have gone off the boil. Profit margins may be important here. You can do simple margin sums by dividing pre-tax profits into sales or turnover (effectively the same thing). If other companies in the same industry are making fatter margins, ask yourself why. It might be that your company is inefficient, or there might be one or two bad bits making losses, or tiny returns, tucked away among the good parts. Either way, unless they are in shrinking industries, they could be attractive to a livelier competitor, who might want to buy the turnover to boost margins (and profits) to his own level, or perhaps simply to close down or sell the loss-makers.

### Capital returns

Returns on capital are trickier. Retailers are fond of checking how many square feet of trading space their rivals own, and calculating sales per square foot. If they themselves get a higher return, they may be interested in bidding. This is the sort of logic behind the Burton bid for Debenhams, and the Dixons bid for Currys and then Woolworth. Others look at brand names, which are often in the balance sheet at nominal value. They calculate their worth under different management, with more aggressive attention to maximizing profits, or perhaps with greater investment in new products under established names. One company paid a fortune for the old 'Bush Radio' name, to slap it on goods imported from the Far East.

### Tired families

Families who have controlled a company for years and have lost their touch are also fair game for bidders. Sometimes the younger generation does not follow into the business, and the original directors opt out and look for a bidder to allow them to cash in and slip quietly into retirement. It is hard, however, to distinguish between large holders who are determined to hang on, and those ready to go.

### Bomb-blasted businesses

Bomb-blasted businesses are really our old friends, the recovery stocks, in a slightly different guise. A bad year or two may have shattered the share price, and the incumbent management may lack the verve or nerve to put the business back together again. Look for companies which have grown fat with assets, have over-expanded through the years or are bowed down by loss-makers and heavy borrowings. You may see that the strength of the assets outweighs the problem areas. There may be opportunities for selling either good businesses to slash borrowings, or bad ones to eliminate losses. If the borrowings come down, the interest burden can be lifted, and profits may leap.

Take Marley, a classic asset-rich company which hit trouble in 1985. Crisis management under banker Sir Robert Clark opted to sell the successful Payless DIY stores, and revitalize the group balance sheet by getting rid of £80 million of borrowings.

### Share stakes

Many bidders telegraph their intentions by picking up a share stake in their victim before they actually bid. Watch the City pages for news of share stakes. As soon as they appear, there will be a flurry of interest, and the price will rise. If the company looks right, go in then. Or if nothing happens in the next few months, you might be able to buy cheaply on a dull day.

Try to go for shares in companies with around the average price/earnings ratio for their sector and with reasonable trading prospects. That way, you might be able to ride the bid roundabout without an additional entry fee. Even if the first stakeholder does not bid, there is always the chance that he will sell to another bidder. Once a stake has been announced, there are always chances – if no bid appears, you will still get periodic bursts of action in the shares, as the market speculates that something is about to happen.

### Leaks

In theory, bids should come like a bolt from the blue. In practice, illegal or not, insiders get to work in four out of five bids, and nibble at the shares. The financial press, especially the market reports in the likes of the *Daily Mail*, are the best guide. Watch, too, for shares which keep hitting new highs or hold steady on days when all about them are falling. Someone knows.

Study reported comments on bid rumours. 'No comment' is pretty imperturbable, but it is astonishing how often company representatives give a clue, wittingly or not. Any reservation at all can be the sign of an honest person who cannot admit what is afoot but will not offer a bare-faced lie. Even so, bare-faced lies do pop out from time to time. The most vehement denial may not be the end of the story: it may be a deliberate attempt to mislead; or it may be that the press is ahead of events – the company itself has not yet learned of the bid which is on its way.

You are on dangerous ground, though, buying bid stocks on the basis of leaks from friends in the business. If your source knows for sure, it is illegal for him to tell you, and illegal for you to deal. If he does not know for sure, you could be buying shares which are being run up by market men who are spreading rumours so that they can sell. You could be buying a pup.

## WHAT TO DO WHEN THE BID COMES

If you have shares when a bid comes, hallelujah! Life is bright and beautiful. Sit back, and enjoy it. You may be bombarded with circulars, but the more the merrier. The more attention you receive, the higher the winning bid is likely to be. Until the closing stages, all you need to worry about is the Monopolies Commission, but these days, most bidders seek guidance first, and do not bid unless they are likely to escape a Monopolies reference. The system is not infallible, however, and some bids do fail. If a reference looks likely, sell straight away; otherwise, do nothing until the last possible moment.

The waiting game is the way to play a bid. Make your decision just before the last closing date, never by the first. Once a bidder has sent out an offer document to shareholders, he has 60 days. If he has not won by then, he cannot try again for a year. Nowadays, though, counter-bidding and general jiggery-pokery introduce all manner of complexities, and bid tussles can go on for months and months.

You should act eventually, however. Do not let a bid slip by without doing something – unless, of course, the bid is for shares in the kind of shell company we touched on earlier. If he chooses, the successful bidder can force you to sell him your shares once he has acceptances from over 90 per cent of the amount of share capital for which he is bidding. Watch this because, by then, you will probably have no option but to take the shares he is offering. His cash alternative, if there was one, may have been withdrawn.

### Taking the cash bid

Your tax position will probably be the most important factor in deciding whether to take cash or shares in a bid. Once you take cash, you have effectively sold, and have thus incurred a capital gains tax liability. This will only matter if your gains in that tax year are above the annual allowance (£6300 for 1986–7). Before you choose cash, check the market price. The value of the bidder's paper (i.e. shares) offer may have pushed the shares above the cash offer, so you might do better selling in the market.

### Accepting shares in a bid

If you accept shares in a bid, you defer your liability to capital gains tax until you sell those shares, and this can be a big advantage. You need to be sure, however, that the shares are worth keeping. Look to see the price the cash alternative puts on the shares you are being offered. This will give you an idea of what the institutions think the shares are worth, because they will probably be underwriting them. They will not want to see them fall below that level.

Check, too, what your income will be if you take shares. Most bids give some form of fixed-interest stock as part of the offer, to ensure that shareholders do not end up with a lower income by accepting. If income is what you want, you might sometimes do better by taking the cash and re-investing in other high yielders.

### Turning down a bid

At times, you might think it worth backing the defence, and turning down a bid. Most shareholders feel a certain allegiance to their directors, and take more notice of them than of the bidder. The defending board will produce a flurry of promises, and the City will expect them to keep them. Usually, shares in a company which has fought off a bid fall when the bid is over, but if the board has put up a strong enough case, they can attract a permanently higher rating. In many cases, the original bidder, or perhaps another, pops up again later.

## BUYING WHEN A BID ARRIVES

No matter how dedicated a detective you might be, you cannot spot bid stocks to order. Do not despair. If you have the nerve – and usually you do not need very much nerve – you can still do well buying bid stocks after the bid arrives. This has become increasingly popular as merger mania has gripped the market's imagination. It has been fuelled by the exploits of the American wheelers and dealers, men such as T. Boone Pickens and Ivan Boesky. They have come unstuck for a few million here and there, but have made hundreds of millions by buying big stakes in companies after a bid has been announced – but before it is all over.

Their financial muscle has allowed them to help dictate events. The small investor cannot hope to do that, but the majority of bids from 1984 onwards have been settled at above the first offer. Almost always, the original bidder has been forced to pay more, or a counter-bidder has topped the lot. There is ample scope for a well-judged speculation after the first offer is announced. The chances of making perhaps a fairly large profit are good. At least you are assured of action.

## WHAT BID LANGUAGE REALLY MEANS

Obviously an agreed bid is of no use: there is no reason for the shares to rise above the bid price, no chance of extra profit. However, most bids are disputed, and the more bitterly, the better. So you need to read between the lines when the combatants start talking.

Under the rules of the Takeover Panel, bidders are not allowed to describe their offer as 'final' until near the very end. Before then, there is always the chance of them paying more, no matter how much they huff and puff. In fact, there is an almost automatic assumption that any first bid is a sighting shot, meant to draw the defence and to measure more accurately what it might take to win. So disregard what the bidder says, until he says his offer is final.

Almost any bid which is not announced as having been agreed at the very beginning will turn into a battle. The first statement from the target company will give an important clue to their attitude. If it follows almost immediately after news of the offer, and talks about inadequate, unsuitable terms, they are planning a tough fight. If the first response takes a day or two, or simply advises shareholders to do nothing for the moment, that means a fight is on, but perhaps the defender is not in such a strong position – they need to think carefully before blasting off.

As ever, the financial press is a crucial source of information. Look for news that the two sides have had preliminary talks. If they had, and the bidder is going ahead, the fight could be really bitter. The two sides have already established that they cannot agree. Watch, too, for any hint of another bidder, or a white knight – a friendly counter-bidder.

Try to judge the emphasis on independence, and whether there is a hint of readiness to sell to someone other than the actual bidder. Check whether the bidder already has a share stake, or if there are other stakeholders who might enter the battle. Watch how many shares the defending directors control, and whether they really count. Certain institutions have a habit of supporting boards – Britannic Assurance (strong in Midlands engineering companies) and unit trust group M & G are especially well known for this. The more shares which look like backing the board, the more likely it is that the bidder will have to pay more.

Directors have a natural inclination to fight to keep their jobs. That angle serves the interests of their shareholders, provided it does not get out of hand. In the end, however, they have an obligation to take a good bid and the institutions will recognize this. The institutions themselves must also operate in the best interests of their shareholders and policyholders.

The victims most likely to put up a strong fight or attract another bid are the best companies. The fatter the asset backing, the bigger the bid. The better the profits record, the higher the value of the company. Any bid should automatically offer a premium for control, so any company should expect to be taken out for at least 1½ times the average price/earnings ratio for the sector.

## THE BANKERS TO BACK

Last, but by no means least, is the identity of the victim's merchant bank. League tables change. In 1985, Morgan Grenfell were top: their reputation took a bash or two in 1986, but if they are acting for the defence, so much the better. Other good names to have on your side include Kleinwort Benson, S. G. Warburg, Hill Samuel, J. Henry Schroder Wagg, N. M. Rothschild, Lazard Brothers and Charterhouse. Close behind come the likes of County Bank, Barclays Merchant Bank, Robert Fleming, Samuel Montagu, Barings, Lloyds Merchant Bank and Hambros.

## THE BIG BAD MONOPOLIES COMMISSION

The one real blot on the horizon is the Monopolies Commission. Bidders rarely give up and walk away, and buy a bid stock at up to 10 per cent over the value of the first bid, and you will rarely come to much harm. However, a reference to the Monopolies Commission usually means bye-bye bid, and it will be at least six months before the bidder can swing back into action, if the Monopolies Commission decides to allow the deal. Inventive merchant bankers have devised ways around this threat, but it can still be nasty. The press is usually quick to weigh up the chances of a Monopolies reference. Do not gamble when there is a chance of a reference.

# 11   The Streetwise Share Trader

Learning about the stock market and share trading never stops. Commit every line, every comma of this book to heart, and you will be on the way to making a killing in the share jungle. The more you understand the theory, the better. There are guides galore to how things ought to work, but they are no substitute for experience and for the personal touch which only you can add.

All along, I have tried to flesh out the theory with insight into what really happens, some of the tricks of the trade. What you need to become is streetwise, alert to everything around you, alive to the impact of everyday events on companies and their share prices. After a while, it becomes natural, instinctive. The streetwise share trader develops a feel for the way people react, the way prices react, how the most routine developments – and the most unlikely matters – can influence companies.

## BACKING THE RIGHT MAN

It takes no great genius to realize that backing the right man is a formula for successful investment. It has come up several times already, especially when we dealt with shell companies and reconstructions, but it matters just as much in big companies as in small ones. Witness the radical impact of Sir John Harvey-Jones upon Imperial Chemical Industries. Before his election as chairman, many thought ICI was already doing pretty well, and represented much that was best in British industry. But Sir John, with his straggly hair, garish kipper ties and energetic, abrasive style, soon showed that there was much that could be changed for the better.

In the High Street, the impact of Sir Terence Conran has made a fortune for those who backed him from his beginnings with Habitat (now merged with British Home Stores to form Storehouse). Sir Ralph Halpern of Burton Group is another High Street hero. Lord Hanson and Sir Gordon White have worked wonders at Hanson Trust. Behind every successful company is a driving personality or two at the top.

The earlier you can spot them, the better. In 1985 there were big profits to be made in the shares of big companies, but the real flyers were the small- to medium-size companies, just getting up speed. A big company whose shares double in a year has done brilliantly, but it is unlikely to do it again the next year. Pick the right man in the right small company, and you could see the price double or treble in the first year, and again in the next. Obviously, though, the smaller company is riskier.

## USING YOUR INSTINCTS

Sorting the prospective high flyer from the common or garden director is not easy. Follow your instincts. If what he says and does seems sensible, back him. If it does not, do not be persuaded. Instinct and common sense are great investment tools. Time and again, they prove to be winners. No matter what others may say, if the new hero strikes you as a shifty character who never gives a straight answer, keep clear.

Every con-man has to have a story, has to be able to persuade people to believe in him if he is going to be able to rip them off. This may sound unduly cynical, the sour reaction of a hard-bitten financial journalist, and perhaps it is. In 25 years of reporting financial affairs, I have met many company promoters who have come unstuck, who were either out to take unsuspecting shareholders for a ride or who were simply not competent to deliver the delights they promised. Every one of them had a fan club and appeared to know all of the answers. So they should. No investor on the outside can understand the inside of a company as well as the person in charge.

Often the promoters themselves believe what they are saying, as they are saying it. They have a shining faith in themselves and their schemes. Step back and think about what they are saying, however, and sometimes the cracks begin to appear.

My scepticism is hard-earned. I have listened to the promises, and watched the problems break in their wake. And read letters from disillusioned investors who have lost their savings. After a while, believing becomes the most difficult thing of all.

The winner is the boss you *can* believe in. You need someone with personality and a plan, someone who makes sense, someone ambitious and someone whose own fortunes depend on the success of the company.

81

Time and again, it comes down to instinct. Never neglect it. Never give the suspect the benefit of the doubt. Always err on the side of caution. No matter how glittering the prize may appear, there will always be another one.

## THE ANNUAL MEETING

Once you have backed your chosen high flyer and bought the shares, make an effort to meet him. The annual meeting is your best opportunity, and you should try to attend. It is the one occasion each year when this captain of industry is answerable to you as a shareholder, one of the owners of the company.

You may be unsure about confronting some well-known name, a man of power and repute. Grit your teeth. He will be nervous, too. Company directors are used to telling others what to do, and a shrewdly framed question at an annual meeting can catch them off guard. Many rehearse their answers, with advisers shooting tricky questions at them before the meeting, especially if something controversial is on the agenda.

Do not be put off. Do not be rude. Be polite, but be firm. Frame your question with a compliment. Listen to the answer. If it does not make sense, or avoids the question, do not hesitate to come back. All too often, shareholders are overcome by nerves, too shy to pick up obvious evasions of their questions. Do not let it happen to you. If it does, learn from it. Ask yourself if you should trust this man with your money.

Make any question brief, clear and to the point. It does not have to be clever; a simple question about progress may be enough. Anything sensible will make a mark, and the chances are that the chairman or some director will want to talk to you about it afterwards. Always stay behind after meetings, and chat to as many directors as you can about the company's affairs. It gives you an excellent chance of weighing up the people who are looking after your investment. If they do not treat sensible questions in a sensible fashion, beware.

## USING YOUR EYES AND EARS

Many companies use annual meetings to display their products and services, and this can give a valuable feel for what is really going on, and can help day-to-day investment judgements. It is routine for the streetwise share trader. You can stumble across the best share tips anywhere, anytime, if you are alert to them.

The transformation of the stuffy old menswear group J. Hepworth into high-flying fashion chain Next happened in the High Street where anyone could see. Drab Hepworth shops closed, and the clean, trendy lines of Next replaced them. A casual glance at the fashion spreads in the papers confirmed that Next boss George Davies was a man to watch. If you backed him near the beginning, it was easy to multiply your money five-fold.

No one needed telling about Laura Ashley, of course, as her designs caught on all around. Record fans who noticed the Our Price shops opening everywhere or watched their regular television commercials could have picked a winner quickly. If you bought an Amstrad word processor (I am writing this on one) soon after the launch, or read reviews of the machine, you would have known that Amstrad were on to a winner which might send the shares soaring. Less obviously, anyone who shopped for food regularly might have wondered at the increasing emphasis on fresh fruit and vegetables in supermarkets, and realized that companies such as Albert Fisher, Glass Glover or Hunter Saphir were doing very nicely out of it.

Was there a message in the flurry of advertisements for personal computers in the early 1980s? Of course. The market was flooded, competition got tough and companies went to the wall. The miners' strike did more than hit the makers of pit props: it also choked house sales in mining areas. And the US bombing of Libya and subsequent fears of terrorist attacks in Europe brought a rush of cancellations in top London hotels from American tourists in 1986. Suddenly the bloom went off Trusthouse Forte.

Share tips – to buy or to sell – are all around, if you can recognize them.

## LISTENING TO THE GOSSIP

Gossip may come your way at your local, or from neighbours on the train. A friend of a friend said chaps from another company have been looking around the works, or a new plant is being built, or a massive order is on the way, or Uncle was told by someone who works in the City that someone is planning a bid – but don't pass it on.

Do not trust the tip. By all means, try to check it, but careless talk costs money. Employees are rarely good at judging the impact of events, real or imaginary, on the shares in their company. Sometimes directors can be hopeless. They may be out of touch with the market. They may not know what the City is expecting, whether what looks a big development to them means much in share-price terms, or whether it has been known for months to the boys in brokers' offices.

Bid whispers may be right – who knows? More often than not, they are wrong. Anyone who really knows about a bid also knows that to tell anyone about it as a tip to buy shares is illegal insider trading. It happens – but such information rarely goes beyond a tight circle of City players. If it does, the odds are that the shares have already moved, because the City insiders heard it first. You could be Tail-end Charlie, the last mug buyer.

Perhaps the one significant exception is where information has been released to unions for their comment. This should not go outside, but it does. More often than not, this is a warning of bad news, of trouble and cutbacks. So be careful. Best rely on your stockbroker for share gossip. That can be pretty unreliable, too, but at least he has some idea of whether it matters to the share price.

## WHAT THE CHAIRMAN REALLY MEANS

There is something about running a public company that brings out the pomposity in people. Even the most down-to-earth directors can get a touch of the pretentious when they write to shareholders in the name of the company. The words get in the way of what they mean to say.

In addition, the bewildering array of Stock Exchange, Takeover Panel and Companies Act rules can nowadays make merely opening your mouth an offence. Or perhaps there is something to hide. Either way, you need to decode the message, or perhaps to clarify it in a chat after the annual meeting.

The future is what is important. Look hard at anything under the heading of 'Prospects' for reservations or modifications. They will not be there by accident. Talk of 'continuing growth' could refer to sales, trading profits, pre-tax profits or earnings. What matters most is earnings. 'Expansion' is another vague word. Does it mean issuing lots of shares? Or will existing businesses do better? If there was heavy capital spending last year, will it bring higher profits this year?

If there is no mention of growth, will there be any? Chairmen should give some guidance, either in the report, or at the annual meeting. What is left unsaid could be more important than what is said. Talk of rationalization means that some part of the business is not going well. Will there be an exceptional charge? Will it be taken above the line (out of pre-tax profits and earnings per share) or below it (from reserves, when analysts might not worry so much)?

Mention of 'increased competition' almost invariably means lower margins and falling profits. Does it mean actual losses? 'Market share' can be tricky, too. Is the market itself growing? Or is the company battling to hold sales in a falling market, while market share rises? 'Currency changes' may influence profits, and could mean assets have to be written down – or up. If the message is not clear to you, never hesitate to ask.

## TALKING TO YOUR BROKER

Talking to your stockbroker, if you have one, can be an art in itself. Never forget that like everyone else, he has an angle. He lives on the commission he earns by buying and selling shares, so he likes you to trade. He also lives on capital gains from trading shares himself, so there are times when it will suit him for you to buy a particular share to help push the price up. And since the Big Bang, the shares he suggests you buy might be owned by his firm – though he will have to tell you.

If he does come up with such an idea, ask why you should buy. There may be a written report from the research department, with profit projections, dividend forecasts, price/earnings ratios and such. Talk to the analyst and note what he says. Ask where the shares are coming from, and how many there are. If they are part of a large line, perhaps someone interesting – a director or a major shareholder – is selling. Why?

In general, it is not a good idea to trade on your broker's gossip, unless you know him extremely well. A new boy, anxious to impress, may give you his best ideas, but his inexperience may tell. A more senior broker will give his best ideas to his biggest clients first. And remember, brokers take less risk themselves when they deal, because they pay no commission, and are in touch with the market minute by minute. Today's favourite may be old news for them tomorrow; they may have been in and out and moved on, while you are still wondering what is happening.

If you contact your broker with an idea, ask what he thinks and what his research department thinks. You may get a frosty response if you are a small trader, but it is worth trying. Ask him to check the price and number of shares traded with all of the jobbers or market-makers (prices may differ from place to place), though a good broker will do this automatically. (Market-makers are the new-fangled equivalent to jobbers after the Big Bang.)

85

## SETTING LIMITS

Always give your broker clear instructions as to how many shares you want and what you want to pay. Be sure whether he is to deal 'at best' – the best price he can get – or 'on limits'. If you set limits, make them clear, and be prepared not to trade if he cannot meet them. Sometimes he will be able to leave your limits with the jobber or market-maker, perhaps for days, and deal if the price hits them. This gives dealers a useful target, and can help get you a better price, but it does not always work.

Make it clear, too, whether your broker can deal at his discretion, or only on your instructions. A good broker can save you money by trading quickly if he sees an opportunity. But you need to trust each other, and it is no good giving your broker discretion, and complaining if his judgement turns out to be wrong.

## NARROW MARKETS

Never buy more shares than the jobber or market-maker will normally quote a price for. If you do, you may find it difficult, when you come to sell, to get out at the market price, especially if prices are falling. If the price is for 5000 shares, do not buy 10,000 unless you are ready to take an extra risk, and prepared to be patient getting out.

If the jobbers quote a price for a relatively small number of shares, with a wide spread between the buying and the selling price – say, more than 4 per cent – take extra care. You have found a narrow-market stock.

This can be magic when the price is rising, for then it responds sharply to modest buying orders. Whereas you can trade in £250,000 worth of ICI shares without shifting the price more than a penny or two, there are shares which move 5 per cent or more on an order worth £1000, and many move by 5 per cent on deals of £5000. These are generally in small, speculative companies.

Narrow-market shares are, however, killers when the price turns down, and this usually happens more swiftly than a rise. The moment they sense sizable selling, the jobbers mark the price down sharply.

It is a brave, or a foolish, investor who weighs in heavily to a narrow-market stock. Seeing it go up, it is tempting to buy more, but be warned. The real disaster for the gamblers in the slump of 1974 was finding that they literally could not sell some shares at any price. If your broker says your favourite stock is a narrow market, think again. Walk away unless you really are ready to walk on the wild side.

## CHEAP AT THE PRICE

Hard to believe, but there are brokers who will peddle you the line that shares are cheap because they were once much dearer. Perhaps weariness makes them do it. Do not get caught. If you study the highs and lows and see a share that is 100p below its peak, it is tempting to think it might go back up again. After all, somebody did once pay that 100p extra. They must have thought it right at the time. Perhaps the price slipped back by chance?

Forget it. Shares do fall out of favour, and prices do suffer from neglect at times, but there is usually a reason. Somebody else knows it. If that price goes back towards the old peak, there will be sellers on the way, relieved to break even and write off a mistake cheaply.

## LISTEN TO THE PRICE

Listen to what the share price is telling you. It is a valuable lesson. Before you buy, watch the price for a while. Get a feel for the range it trades in, how sharply it rises, how sharply it falls. Pay special attention to the way it behaves on days of unusual market activity. If it falls when all else is rising, be wary. If it holds steady, or edges higher when others are falling, someone is confident enough to pick it up through thick and thin. Smart dealers know how to build a share stake without attracting attention. They try to buy when the market is falling, lay off for a while to let sellers come in, and pick the stock up again if it falls.

Get your broker to try to check with the jobber or market-maker. A good broker may be able to wheedle out whether the buying is from a consistent source. He may even get some idea of the sort of dealing limits in operation. When the big boys are buying, you may be able to tag along for a ride.

Shares tend to get a momentum going. Do not fight it. If a share keeps sliding gently, be suspicious. If you are determined to buy, wait for it to find a level. It is worth sacrificing 10 per cent or so to make sure the fall is over. Let someone else risk buying at the bottom. Equally, there are times when a rise goes steadily on and up. It is always hard to guess where it will stop. Stay aboard while it lasts, if you can time it correctly – which brings us to charts and chartists.

# DOUBLE BOTTOMS AND PLUNGING NECKLINES – THE CHARTS

There are people who live by charts, who swear they tell you the true share story. They shut their eyes to fundamentals – such things as profits and dividends – watch dots or crosses on graph paper, and reckon the real action is there, plain to see.

It is easy to mock. One of the noisiest names in the business used his charts to recommend one company less than a fortnight before the receiver moved in. Had he spoken to brokers who followed the company, or looked at the accounts, he would have known what a desperate state the firm was in before he wrote. Now he checks the fundamentals before going overboard on chart tips.

There is, however, another side to the coin. Jim Slater was asked at one annual meeting of Slater Walker what he thought of chartists who said his shares were too high. He answered scornfully that chartists tended to have ragged raincoats and big overdrafts. A few years later, Slater Walker crashed.

Charts can be a valuable aid, if you are first sure of the investment basics. They do give an idea of what other investors think, and sometimes show what the insiders are doing. Once you have found a sound share, there is no harm in seeing what the chartists say. Most brokers have one tucked away somewhere. And you can watch for their views in the financial press, or in specialist services.

*What chartists do*

Chartists draw patterns around share-price moves. Some follow the closing price each day, marking it on a vertical scale, with the time period on the horizontal. Others make bar charts, placing a little vertical line to cover the high and low trading range for the day, with a horizontal line for the closing level.

Point and figure charts are more ambitious. These focus on significant price movements, with a vertical row of crosses for each worthwhile gain, and noughts for each fall. There is no set time-scale. A new column is formed with each change of direction.

The chartist seeks a pattern in the dots or lines. A double bottom shows a price falling to a low, then rising, and finally falling back to that low. That might mean the shares will go no lower. It might mean someone is buying at a particular level, and this the chart watcher can follow.

On the other hand, a double bottom might become a triple bottom.

Or even a false bottom, followed by a lower bottom. Turn bottoms upside down, and they become tops – points at which shares stop rising, and a seller always seems to hit the price.

Plunging necklines catch the chartist's eye in a falling market. A neckline is a support level established below a head-and-shoulders formation. Leave it to the experts to establish what that is, along with flags, spear points, rectangles, reverse heads and shoulders, and other exotica.

Around all of these, chartists draw conclusions about trends and momentum. Ask about them, and you may be told that a trend is a trend until it stops. That sums up a great deal about chart watching. It may tell you what is going on, but is of limited use for what you really want to know – what is going to happen next.

## The value of charts

Charts do have a value, however, because a number of people pay attention to them. No matter how daft it may seem, anything which influences prices is important if it prompts people to buy or sell. Talk about support points and resistance levels means that the chartists think it will be important if a share – or perhaps the market – moves beyond a particular level. They may be telling clients that if the *Financial Times* Index falls below 1250, an important support level has been breached, and a slump may follow. Some clients may take notice and sell, so the prediction becomes self-fulfilling. You may not heed it, but it is as well to be aware of what is going on.

Charts are handy, too, to show what people have been paying for shares. And to give an idea of the likely supply of buyers or sellers. If a lot of people bought shares around a particular price, it matters. Usually the charts show where it has happened, with the price hovering around that level for a long while. When a price is falling, it may form a *support point*, showing the price at which investors are more prone to buy.

Where a share is rising, signs on the chart that it once hovered above a particular price may indicate a potential *resistance level*, where many bought earlier, saw a fall and may get out when they get their money back. It may be significant if the price goes above this resistance level: potential sellers may be finished, and future buyers will find the shares in shorter supply, so they will rise more rapidly. In a falling market, the reverse may happen: if a share drops through a support point, where there have been ready buyers in the past, potential new buyers may be put off, and sellers will hit the price harder.

Such an outline does scant justice to what has become a very sophisticated game, but it will suffice for many investors. Chartists would be more convincing if they could agree on the meaning of charts. Ask half-a-dozen of them about the same chart, and you may get six very different views. That, as they say, is what makes a market.

### Insider dealing – the chart to watch

There is, however, one chart service well worth watching. It is called 'Strategic Holdings for Take-overs' (available from B.R.I. Information Services Ltd, 18 Brooks Road, Sutton Coldfield, West Midlands B72 1HP), and it monitors how the directors have been buying and selling their shares. The *Daily Mail* reports on it from time to time, and so does the *Sunday Times*. By monitoring every directors' share trade, it focuses on one of the virtues of charts: they help pick out odd price moves which might be overlooked. Sometimes these are the result of well-informed dealing, not by directors but by others who know full well what is happening. Often, these moves take place when there is no clue for those who track investment fundamentals alone.

## NO ONE LEFT TO BUY

Charts can help clarify some of the rules the professionals keep in mind, especially those relating to the particular characteristics some shares develop. It all goes back to instinct, developing a feel for the market. Watch, and you will observe how some shares never make much progress, no matter how impressive the fundamentals.

Year in, year out, analysts used to estimate that the asset value of the multinational Lonrho was four or five times greater than the share price, that profits were rising and that the dividend yield was into double figures, way above the average. Nevertheless, investors remained unimpressed and the shares stuck in a narrow trading range.

In the City, you either loved Lonrho chief Tiny Rowland or hated him. In 1985, though, Lonrho began to break out of the rut, and the shares powered ahead in the second half of 1985, and on into 1986. After years of stagnation, they had found a new generation of buyers, young fund managers ready to buy a high-yielding stock without prejudice from long-established City doubts about the company. Until then, all of the believers had the shares, and the rest did not want to know. There was no one left to buy, not matter how bright the prospects appeared.

Shares do run out of buyers. They become accustomed to their rating. The market grows used to some shares on low price/earnings ratios, and others on high ones, and tends to leave them there indiscriminately. It can take a major change to shift the traders' perceptions. Do not fight it. Only the big players will change this situation. Spot when they start, and you can enjoy the ride. Until you are sure it is happening, stay away.

## LATE NEWS

Be wary too, of company announcements which come late. Bad figures almost invariably take longer to add up than good ones. Companies sometimes announce in advance the date on which they will publish profit statements, but there is no clear rule. Usually, however, any such announcements are made at about the same time each year, so keep an eye on your diary. Any profit statement which is more than three weeks overdue by comparison with the previous year's date should be viewed with suspicion. Ask your broker if he knows the reason for the delay. Or try ringing the company secretary. It might be safest not to wait, if you get uncertain answers, and to sell before the company says anything officially.

## ONE PRODUCT COMPANIES

Take special care with one product companies, or companies which depend for a large slice of their business on one customer. When the competition comes along, as surely it will eventually, they can crumble fast.

# 12   Selling shares

It is easy to buy a share, harder to sell it. Somehow parting with an investment seems to be a much more emotional affair than picking it in the first place. Investors can be remarkably patient with a tipster who gets it wrong and goes for a dud. Tell someone to take profits on a favourite when it goes up, and the complaints come loud and long. Hell hath no fury like a winner scorned.

Selling, though, is the essential second half of successful investment. It is no good spotting winner after winner if you are holding on when the market turns, and everything tumbles out of bed, good with bad. The only profits which count are the ones you take, the ones you bank by selling winners while you are ahead. Paper profits are for the birds.

The classic investment rule is to cut losses quickly, and let your profits run. Everybody knows that. Most investors ignore it. There is a natural tendency to sell winners to finance the losers. Surprisingly many investors are patient with their duds, reluctant to accept that they have got it wrong and that the best way out is the quickest.

## CUTTING YOUR LOSSES

DO IT. Cut your losses. Investment experts count themselves content if they pick six winners out of ten – anything better is a bonus. That may be a trifle conservative in a bull market, but it is not altogether unrealistic. If you can pick more winners than losers, you should come out ahead. You will certainly come out ahead if you make it an unbudging rule to sell losers while the losses are small, and hold winners while the profits are piling up.

It is obvious, so elementary that it hardly needs saying. Years of talking to investors, reading their letters, listening to their excuses make it plain that few people heed it. CUT, CUT, CUT YOUR LOSSES QUICKLY.

Everyone will have their own ideas of what cutting losses quickly means. Time does not matter. Linger as long as you like, but move swiftly once the loss starts to appear. It sounds like a cop-out, but it is best to set yourself a target. Promise yourself to sell if your shares fall beyond a certain point, and set this point (called a 'stop-loss level') when you buy. Set it sensibly: make it between 10 and 20 per cent below your buying level, less if you are an aggressive investor.

No one buys a share with the idea of losing, but the sensible investor admits the possibility. Keep a stop-loss figure in mind. Ask your broker. Some will accept stop-loss levels, and will try to operate them. Others may rely on you to tell them. Ask.

## THE STOP-LOSS SYSTEM

Careful investors will go further than simply placing a stop-loss order on losers. Although it takes some of the romance and fun out of investment, eliminating the thrill of driving brilliantly by the seat of your pants, a fully fledged stop-loss system to cover all sales – on winners and losers – has a great deal to commend it. Despite its name, such a system can be used to preserve profits, and ensure that they do not just slip away.

It may sound a trifle complicated, but once you get used to the idea, it is simplicity itself. It also has the virtue of encouraging you to watch prices day by day, so that you develop a greater feel for what is happening.

When you buy a share, set a price at which you will sell should it fall, as with the simple stop-loss plan outlined above. As the price rises, move your potential selling price up behind it – a 'trailing stop-loss'. Never cheat. Never, ever lower your stop-loss price.

Say you buy at 100p. Set your first stop-loss price at 80p. Sell if it falls that far. If the price rises to 110p, raise your stop-loss level to 90p. If the price rises to 120p, trail your stop-loss up behind it to 100p. And so on. If the price gets to 150p, your stop-loss price should be 130p. If there is a market slump, or something goes wrong in the company, you will have clinched a 30 per cent profit by selling at 130p. You may have missed the top, but you will not be left miserable, with no profit at all, if the price settles back to 100p.

The disadvantage is obvious – you never get out at the top. And selling at the top gives a really warm glow. Remember, though, the old Rothschild maxim: he made his fortune by selling too soon, but he sold at a profit.

The system is not infallible – no system is. There are times when it

93

will take you out of super stocks too soon; it may take you out of a potential winner at a loss, before it takes off. On balance, though, it will ensure that you come out ahead, provided you pick more winners than losers. It will make all of your losses little ones, and some of your profits should be big.

It also helps to guard against your natural weakness. Unless you are an exceptional investor, you will be tempted to hang on to losers too long, and to sell your winners to finance losers for a second chance. Do not do it. Let the system take away the temptation. It works.

In the 1970s, I edited a tip sheet. Many shares I recommended multiplied five-, six-, seven-fold, but several of the most successful disappeared in the secondary banking crash. The stop-loss system should have taken subscribers out within 20 per cent of the peak; no one should have been holding on when the companies went to the wall. I hope every subscriber took the stop-loss system seriously and followed it.

## AVERAGING

Now and then, the idea of averaging intrudes upon the investment scene, and it is particularly popular among unit trust managers in uncertain markets. What fun, the story goes, to spend a set amount each month. When prices are low, it will buy more units. When prices rise, you will feel the benefit of averaging, with cheap units as well as dear ones.

This has a certain logic if you want a regular savings plan, but it is not to be taken seriously by the sensible share trader. It is simply another way of postponing the decision to take a loss. On the surface, it has an appeal. If you buy 500 shares at 100p each, and another 500 when they have fallen to 50p, then the price only has to rise to 75p for you to be breaking even on your 1000 shares.

Forget it. You should have sold your 100p loser at 80p. If it has halved, something is clearly wrong. It could take an age before the price recovers, and it may go further down.

## PYRAMIDING

The reverse of averaging is pyramiding, but while averaging tends to crop up when shares have fallen, pyramiding is applied to shares which are rising. The idea is that is you buy, say, 500 shares at 100p and they rise to 125p, you should back a winner and buy more. When your first 500 shares hit 125p, you have a paper profit of £125. If you buy another 200 shares at 125p, you will have invested a total of £750, and will have 700 shares, costing an average of just over 107p each. You will still have a profit on the whole lot, thanks to the safety margin built in by your first successful purchase, and you will have more shares to profit from if they keep going up. If they should fall, you have a margin which would allow you to sell out quickly before there is a loss.

It is an aggressive strategy which may appeal to some, but only try it if you are ready to watch prices like a hawk, for these can turn quickly. You could get caught with more shares than you had intended, and a share price tumbling too fast for you to sell while you are ahead. In theory, though, pyramiding has more to commend it than averaging. At least you are trying to back a winner, instead of nursing a loser.

## SELLING HALF

Pick a big winner, and you can end up with one holding which has outgrown your portfolio. While the others have toddled along, one has shot up, and may account for half of your investment total or more. It is a nice problem to have.

The traditional approach says that it *is* a problem, and should be cut down to size. The conventional approach says to take any share which has doubled, and sell half, leaving the other half in your list for nothing.

That is no way to make a killing. There is no reason why you should not ride a winner and see it multiply three, four or more times without selling a single share. If you have been bright enough and lucky enough to pick such a share, stay with it.

Have nothing to do with stick-in-the-mud plodders who would part you from a super share. Once big winners begin to rise, they can go like a rocket. Stay with them while the ride lasts. Think about taking profits when the price starts to falter.

Once again, a stop-loss is useful, but you can cheat a little if you are riding a rocket. Trail the stop-loss price not 20 per cent but 30 per cent behind the price, once it has doubled. Exceptional shares call for exceptional measures. If the price becomes more volatile, allow for a larger setback before selling. With bigger profits, you can afford to be more relaxed.

It makes sense, too, to shift the stop-loss price up more slowly. Let shares settle at higher levels. Sometimes a big rise is quickly followed by a lapse. If you raise the stop-loss level too quickly, you could get taken out too soon.

Follow high flyers very carefully. Once they stop rising, take care. Shares are for buying and selling, not for loving for ever. When a winner falters, start to worry. Watch your stop-loss carefully. If you have widened it to 30 per cent on the rise, close it up as the momentum slackens. You may be able to tolerate a 30 per cent fall while a big winner is moving fast, but once the motion is lost, the fun may be over.

Do not stick with a winner for sentimental reasons. The first big move is the easiest. The greater the gain, the greater the odds against a further big gain. It is worth asking yourself whether you would buy your winner at the higher price. If you would not, perhaps you ought to sell.

Selling to restore balance to a portfolio only makes sense for nervous investors. Investment is not a science, and investors should play the way they feel happiest. There is nothing but common prudence to suggest a spread of investments is right. If you want to gamble on just one or two stocks, do it, but understand that the odds are against you.

## SELL SIGNALS

Unless you have a system, deciding when to sell can be a real problem. No bell rings when a share hits the top. One form of help is to turn upside down the rules you tried to follow when you bought. Ask yourself if the things which attracted you to the company still prevail. If you have done well, the price/earnings ratio will no longer be so low, nor the yield so high. Compare them with the average, and ask yourself if they are too far out of line. Ask yourself if they look attractive to new buyers. You may feel comfortable sitting on a fat profit, but if there is no reason for anyone to buy, the shares are not going to rise any further. Perhaps you should sell.

Time and again, deciding when to sell comes back to using something like a stop-loss system. Much of it is about interpreting what the share price is saying. You do not need a system to understand the fact that, once a share has hit a peak and begins to fall, it has lost momentum. You have to judge how much of a fall you can tolerate before getting out.

*If in doubt, sell out*

It is difficult to strike a balance between short-term profit-taking, and long-term patience. Those who hold out longer are often said to do better than quick in-and-out merchants, but if you are going to sit and wait, you have to be sure you are doing it in the right share. Only you can decide. Err on the side of safety: if in doubt, sell out.

You should not be content to sit with a share which is quietly slipping back while you watch profits ebb away. Put a price or time limit on it. Decide how far you can let the price fall before you will sell, or how long you will wait for a rise. If a price becomes becalmed, then begins to slide, sell. Ask yourself if you could be doing better somewhere else. If you see something which may move more quickly, take your profits and buy it.

If you are awake, the main sell signal usually comes from the share price itself. Watch if it fails to go up, or eases back, when other shares are soaring. Unless you know of a reason for a rise ahead, sell.

*A market slump*

If the whole market is headed for a slump, sell everything, no matter how bright individual prospects appear. Some shares do rise against a falling market, but they are exceptions. Do not risk it. It may not be easy to tell when the whole market is going to slide, but always try to be alive to the possibility. No one buys the whole market, and it is easy to get so caught up in watching individual stocks that a major market slump comes as a shock. If the indices are on the slide – the *Financial Times* 30-Share Index (which covers moves in the shares of 30 leading companies) or the *Financial Times* All-Share Index – and the press is full of predictions of economic gloom, a sterling slump, a change of government or industrial strife, get out. Put your money into a building society until the trouble blows over.

*Watch the competition*

Other selling signs may come from the competition to your favourite company. Keep an eye out for troubles in the industry your company operates in. If one brewer has had a bad summer, most others will be struggling too. If terrorist bombs hit bookings at the Savoy, then Trusthouse Forte will be suffering – and so on. Do not forget allied industries. If house sales flag, worry not just about housebuilders, but also about brickmakers, estate agents and mortgage finance companies.

*Boardroom bust-ups*

A boardroom bust-up can be a sell sign. Generally, though, it is good

97

news. Either the management which stays will get on better, with a united front, or will be more vulnerable to a bid, especially if the board change involves big moves in share stakes.

### Sell ahead of an announcement

Short-term players should be ready to sell ahead of news from the company, rather than after it. The stock market almost always overdoes things. Anticipation is usually the most rewarding part of investment – unless there is a bid. Each Monday or Saturday, most City pages list the main board meetings in the week ahead. Prices frequently rise ahead of those meetings. Check then, and if you are trading for the short term, or thinking of selling anyway, do it before any announcement.

By the time you see it in the newspapers, good news will be known all over the City, and the shares will have reacted. You will often find that others had bought in anticipation, and sell once the news was made public. That is why many shares fall on good news: it would have taken something really extraordinary for a further gain. By selling ahead of the news, too, you avoid any risk of disappointment.

### Selling on a tip

Every now and then, shares take a great leap forward for no apparent reason. You may discover they have been tipped in a newsletter, in the press or by some stockbroker. If a good broker is getting behind them, stay aboard, but if it is a tipsheet or some minor press pundit, read what they say and then make up your own mind if it is a good selling opportunity. For that reason, think twice before selling on a Friday. The weekend press carries a shower of tips, and your share could get a Monday morning boost out of it.

### End-account selling

Friday is rarely a good day to sell, partly because of the weekend press, and partly because it often marks the end of the Stock Exchange account.

The Stock Exchange calendar divides the year into two- or three-week account periods, which normally end on a Friday. Buy and sell inside the account, and you could clinch a profit before you have to pay for your shares. Many professionals trade that way. They have to sell by the end of the account, or keep the shares and pay, so the last Thursday or Friday of an account can be a bad time to sell, because account traders are getting out, the jobbers know it and will mark prices lower accordingly. If you want to sell, try to do it in the first half of the week, all else being equal.

## Sell in May

The market is full of old saws, but some of them make sense. 'Sell in May and go away' is a favourite that, in recent years, has worked more often than not. It has some logic because the City winds down in the summer. People go on holiday, Parliament is quiet, there is Wimbledon, Ascot, Henley and a host of other distractions, with free tickets and parties to tempt fund managers away from their desks. Most companies end their financial year on 31 December or 31 March. The December year-end brigade report profits around March and April, the March year-end profits tend to come by the middle of June. So mid-summer is quieter on the company front. If you do sell in May, think about buying during the second half of August. Business gets back to normal in September.

## Betting against the crowd

'Contrary thinking', or betting against the crowd, is another well-worn City favourite, used as an excuse to buy or to sell. Somehow though, it gains most prominence as a sell signal.

Often it is employed to sneer that when the small investor comes into the market in force, it is time for the sophisticated investor to say goodbye. Although a cliché, it may have some force if applied judiciously: the bigger the crowd, the fewer there are left to join in, and share prices need new converts to buy constantly if they are to continue rising.

However, be careful about betting against the crowd, for the crowd creates the winners. Do take the precaution of looking hard at any bandwagon before you jump aboard. Check where it started: the further it has come, the nearer the end it must be. Try not to be the last one aboard. Sensible contrary thinking should mean that you consider both sides of any situation before making a move.

# SELLING ON THE CYCLE

If you are a believer in business cycles – that boom follows slump and vice versa – you will take them into account in buying and selling decisions. In practice, their stock market muscle corresponds to the number of players who follow them, and that is small.

There are all sorts of cycles. Most popular is the Kondratieff Cycle, advanced by a Soviet academic who died in a Siberian labour camp in the 1930s. There is keen debate over the timing of his 45-to-55-year cycle. It was widely considered that 1984 would be a Kondratieff crunch year; it did not happen. Some predict dire economic events at any moment on the strength of Kondratieff. They have been predicting them, consistently, each year since 1982.

American chartist R. N. Elliott formed the idea that bull (rising) and bear (falling) phases of the stock market come in five up-waves, followed by three down. He threw in a sequence of numbers from a 12th-century mathematician called Fibonacci, and refined them further. All sorts of other systems abound. Until you start hearing their names regularly, do not bother with them. Only when lots of players use them to influence share prices will they matter.

## SELLING SHORT

It is easy to deal with selling short: *do not do it*. Do not even think about it until you have a fat investment fortune to fall back on, and are too sophisticated to need anything this book can tell you.

Professionals can make big money selling short in a falling market. The short seller finds a share he thinks will fall, sells and hopes to buy back at a lower price. He is selling shares he does not own. Sooner or later, he will have to buy them to complete his trade. If they rise, he loses money when he buys. In buying, he helps push the price up against himself if it is not possible to buy the full number in one deal.

See how it works. The short seller sells, say, 1000 shares in ICI at 940p. He does not own those shares. If they then fall to, say, 900p, he can buy 1000 shares to complete the deal. He has made profits of 40p a share, before expenses, or £400. However, if he has sold at 940p, and then ICI shares rise, and he has to buy at 980p so that he can deliver the shares he has contracted to sell, he loses 40p a share, or £400 plus expenses.

When you buy a share, you can only lose as much as you have spent. Sell short, and you cannot tell how much you might lose if you get it wrong. You could sell short of a share at 100p, and be forced to buy it back at 500p – or 1000p. Such extreme examples hardly ever happen, but every now and then, short sellers – the bears – get squeezed very hard.

## THE COVERED BEAR

You can go part of the way to selling short by becoming a 'covered

100

bear'. The covered bear picks a company in which he holds shares, sells an equivalent number to those he holds and hopes he can buy them back at a lower price. If they do not fall, he is covered because he can call on the shares he owns, completing his bargain by delivering them. It only makes sense if you expect the shares you are holding to take a temporary dip and then recover quickly. Otherwise you should sell the lot and forget them.

# 13   Gilts, Loans and Option Games

There are things on the Stock Exchange which are not shares. More than three quarters of stock market turnover by value is in government securities. Up to £800 million of them change hands in a single day. When interest rates are moving sharply, they can produce hefty gains or losses for investors, though they are generally presented as the safer end of the Stock Exchange. Through 1985, most government securities traded within a range of ten points – nothing too exciting – but over the first four months of 1986, when interest rates were falling sharply, securities with a life of between five and 15 years commonly scored gains of 20 points or more – heady stuff.

## GILT-EDGED SECURITIES

Government securities are known as gilt-edged securities – gilts, for short – because they are issued by the government, the most reliable borrower of all, the one who (supposedly) can never go bust. Gilts are the prime source of funding for the 'Public Sector Borrowing Requirement' (PSBR), that chunk of jargon which crops up regularly in discussions about where the economy is going. Insurance companies, pension funds and such are the biggest buyers, using them to lock in a guaranteed return to meet future liabilities.

The price of gilts is always so much per £100 of stock, and £100 is the nominal, or par, value. That nominal value has a real meaning for gilts. Unlike the nominal value of a share – which gives no indication of the real worth of that share – the nominal (£100) value of a gilt means that, at or between specific dates, you will be paid £100 by the government for every £100 nominal you hold (except in the case of undated gilts, which may never be repaid). So if in the summer of 1986, you could buy Exchequer 2·5 per cent 1990 stock at £86, you would be repaid at £100 for every £100 nominal in 1990.

## Flat yields

The price of gilts is governed by interest rates: when interest rates fall, gilt-edged prices rise; when interest rates rise, gilt values fall. If you buy a gilt with a 10 per cent coupon (the nominal rate of interest it pays), standing at £100, it gives a flat yield of 10 per cent. If interest rates fall, the gilt may rise in value to, say, £110, where it would yield 9·09 per cent (10 divided by 110, multiplied by 100). If interest rates rise, to say, 12 per cent, then the price of the gilt with a 10 per cent coupon would fall to £83, where it would yield 12 per cent (10 divided by 83 multiplied by 100).

## Redemption yields

Values are complicated, however, by the life of the gilt. Those with a life of up to five years are called 'shorts', those to be redeemed between five and 15 years are 'mediums', and those with more than 15 years to repayment are 'longs'. A small number of stocks, redeemable after a certain date but with no specific redemption date, are called 'undated'; War Loan is the best known of these.

Take, for example, 12·5 per cent Treasury Stock 2003–2005. This has a coupon of 12·5 per cent, and will be repaid at £100 for every £100 nominal between the years 2003 and 2005 (it is safest to assume that repayment will be at the last possible date). Because gilts sell above their £100 nominal value, or below it, according to the relationship between general interest rates and the rate the securities pay, the repayment date is important, and influences their value. This time factor is taken into account, and linked to the flat yield to give the redemption yield. Redemption yield is the most widely used yield for gilts.

Clearly if a stock is standing at £105, and will be redeemed in a year's time at £100, the holder will lose £5 in capital on repayment, and will need extra income to make up for that. Conversely, if a stock is at £95, and will be repaid at £100 in a year's time, the holder will get a capital gain of £5, and can expect to receive less interest because of it. Gains or losses on repayments are effectively incorporated into interest payments to arrive at the redemption yield.

## Tax benefits

The tax position of the purchaser determines where we go from here. Redemption yields are generally quoted gross – without deduction of tax. Only non-taxpayers (oh, there are some) get the full amount. So non-taxpayers will pick stocks with high flat yields. High-taxpayers will plump for low coupon stocks (some have a 2·5 or 3 per cent coupon) that carry a much greater capital gain. Capital gains on gilts are free of tax, whereas income is taxed at the individual's highest rate.

### Index-linked gilts

There is another gilt-edged complication. Since 1985, the Government has been issuing index-linked gilts. These are not redeemable at £100 for every £100 nominal in issue, as with other gilts. Their capital repayment value goes up automatically in line with inflation, as measured by the Retail Price Index. The coupon, or nominal interest rate, is therefore a 'real' return. It may look low, at 2 or 3 per cent, but you actually get that 2 or 3 per cent without having to worry about the inroads of inflation on your capital. And it is inflation that erodes the real worth of other fixed-interest investments.

Because of this, an index-linked gilt may sometimes be more attractive than a conventional gilt with the same coupon. There are index-linked gilts to cover most people's preferred time-span – short, medium or long – and some should be especially attractive to high-taxpayers. However, falling inflation rates have left index-linked gilts behind conventional ones in the race for capital gains in the first year or two of their lives.

### Buying gilts

Trading in gilts may sound terribly complicated, and so it can be. If you want to do it – and there are times when it may offer a haven from a stormy share market – consult a broker who is expert in such matters. Most firms have a clued-up gilt department to help.

If you can manage to do it yourself, however, go to the Post Office. Many gilts can be traded over the counter at larger ones with low dealing commissions. Gilts bought through the Post Office have another important advantage over gilts bought through a stockbroker or a bank: dividends are paid without tax being deducted. This saves complications for low-rate taxpayers, who would otherwise have to go through the ponderous business of reclaiming tax. And it gives you the use of the taxable part of the dividend for longer. You do, though, have to declare it, and pay tax on it in the end.

The gilts available over the counter at Post Offices are listed on what is called the National Savings Stock Register. The commissions charged for buying and selling these are set out below:

| *Size of deal* | *Commission charge (including VAT)* |
|---|---|
| Up to £250 | £1 |
| Over £250 | £1 plus 50p for every extra £125 or part |

| | |
|---|---|
| Less than £100 | 10p for every £10 or part |
| £100 to £250 | £1 |
| Over £250 | £1 plus 50p for every extra £125 or part |

*Gains from gilts*

Gilts have their attractions. Buy them at the right time, and they allow you to lock in a high fixed return with safety, over a long, fixed period. If you buy when interest rates are high, and sell when they are lower, you can also secure sizable capital gains, free of capital gains tax. But there is the threat of inflation, except in index-linked gilts. Get your timing wrong, and you could face capital losses.

However, it should be remembered that buoyant share markets usually take place against a background of steady or rising gilt prices, so when gilts make money, shares are offering opportunities, too. Pick the right share, and you will leave the best gilts standing on capital gains. Unless you think low interest rates and falling inflation are here to stay, do not buy gilts when interest rates are under 8 per cent. You are then likely to be near the bottom of the interest rate range, and could face capital losses when rates rise.

## CONVERTIBLE LOAN STOCKS

There is a halfway house between the sober-sided fixed-interest market and the thrills and spills of Ordinary shares – the convertible loan stock.

Convertible loan stocks carry a fixed rate of interest, a date when they will be redeemed at £100 for every £100 nominal, and the opportunity to convert into Ordinary shares at certain dates. The number of Ordinary shares you can switch into is fixed, and when convertible loan stocks are first issued, the conversion terms normally let you into the Ordinary shares at a premium to the price then. Say, the Ordinary shares stand at 40p in the market when the convertible is first issued. That convertible may allow you to switch in three years' time into 200 Ordinary shares for every £100 of convertible loan stock – equivalent to buying 200 Ordinary shares at 50p each in three years' time. You will not be able to switch right away, but by the time three years is up, the hope is that the Ordinary shares will have risen to 50p, or more.

The best convertibles have a long conversion run – a chance of switching into Ordinary shares over several years – but the first conversion date should not be too far away. You may be able to find convertibles which switch into the Ordinary shares at below the current price, and give a higher yield in the meantime. Sometimes, of course, such apparent bargains signal something wrong. But convertibles do occasionally get overlooked if there is a run in the Ordinary shares, and sometimes a poor market in the convertible lets the price drift out of line. Pick a good one, and you get both capital gains and a good yield.

### Convertible dangers

In general, the notion is that higher income on convertible loan stocks is a shelter from short-term uncertainties in the shares. Be careful. This works sometimes, but weak shares make a weak convertible, and a few points of extra interest is no consolation if your capital value tumbles as the company hits trouble. Never buy a convertible unless you are sure that the shares themselves are worth buying.

This is another area where expert broker advice pays. Make sure you understand the conversion rights properly, as some stocks are only partly convertible, and be sure not to let the convertible go past the last conversion date without switching. You could be left with a boring fixed-interest stock, and that is no joke.

## PREFERENCE PROFITS

Preference stocks are often forgotten and, on the face of it, they have little to offer. They bear a fixed rate of interest, and rank ahead of Ordinary shares in their claim on dividends and on assets when a company is wound up.

The fun starts, though, if a company hits hard times, and suspends preference dividends. Most preference capital is cumulative, which means that holders are entitled to all of the dividends they missed in the bad times before the company could start paying dividends to Ordinary shareholders when times were better. It takes a little nerve, but if you can spot cumulative preference stocks in a company with a generous asset backing whose fortunes are on the turn, you could do very nicely. You could get a big slug of back dividends, or might find the directors want to get rid of the preference capital in a reconstruction, and will repay it at £100 for every £100 nominal.

Most preference stocks trade at well below their nominal value, so any capital reconstruction is likely to mean a fat profit. Preference stocks tend to be overlooked in bid battles. They get taken over in a footnote to the main event at a handsome price. For example, you might be able to buy preference stock at £40 for £100 nominal, and see it repaid at £100 for every £100 nominal.

Preference stocks are not for everyone. They can take years to come good, and they can be difficult to buy and sell, but do not write them off completely.

# WARRANTS

Warrants are a little like convertible loan stocks, without the income. They can offer a super low-cost, long-term gamble.

They usually arrive as part of some bigger refinancing package, and are soon traded separately. They act as long-running options, carrying the right to subscribe for new shares at a set price in the future. In theory, their value is calculated by reference to the price at which they allow the holder to buy new shares, and the date on which those shares can be bought. In practice, the value is determined by supply and demand. Several warrants sell at prices above or below what backroom broking boys impute their worth to be on the mathematical models.

## How warrants can be big winners

If you pay 20p for a warrant to subscribe for one new share at 100p, you are effectively paying 120p for that new share. Generally you will be getting in at a premium over the current market price, which may only be 105p, but the warrants will not allow you to buy those shares until some future date, when they may be well above 120p. The subscription price will not change no matter what, so you will only pay 100p for each of the new shares. If the market price is 200p when the warrant date arrives and you subscribe for them, the warrants then will be worth 100p (200p minus 100p subscription price).

This means that the warrants will have gone up five-fold from the 20p you paid, while the shares have not quite doubled from 105p. The gearing is terrific. You will have done much better in the warrants than in the shares, although you will have missed the dividends to Ordinary shareholders.

A well-chosen warrant can be a big winner. Some run for 10 years or more, giving a low-priced way of buying into a growth company without tying up a lot of capital for a long time. Again, this is a market for the specialist, and the big brokers have departments watching warrants. They are especially popular now among investment trusts, where they offer a long-distance gamble on a general rise in the market through the growth in a trust's spread of share investments.

## TRADITIONAL OPTIONS

Although the glamorous and new traded option market has grabbed the headlines in recent years, traditional options still offer a useful way into shares without laying out a fortune. Options carry the right to buy or sell a share at a set price – the 'striking price' – at some time in the future. Most conventional Stock Exchange options run for three months (or seven Stock Exchange trading accounts). They carry the right to buy ('call options'), to sell ('put options') or to buy or sell ('double options'). The options themselves cannot be bought or sold.

Options can be negotiated in most shares, at a cost of between 8 and 15 per cent of the share price for put or call options, and roughly double that for double options. When you buy them, you pay stockbroking commission on the full value of the shares covered by the option, even if you later abandon the option. However, when you exercise the option, use it – you pay no extra commission.

The cost of an option can only be set off against capital gains for tax purposes if you exercise it, and so sometimes it is as well to exercise an option, even at a small loss.

Options can be expensive, but they do give you control of a lot of stock – far more, perhaps, then you could afford – and let you walk away if you get it wrong, losing only the cost of your option. You do not have to exercise options. Get them wrong, and you cannot lose more than your option money, whatever happens.

### How a call option works

If you believe that, say, GEC will soar in the next three months, buy a call option on 1000 shares. The market price may be 179p to 182p per share, and a call costs 17p for each share. The striking price – that is, the price at which you can buy 1000 GEC in the next three months will be 182p. Add 17p to 182p, plus £35 costs, and you are breaking even when GEC top 202½p. For every 1p that they rise thereafter,

108

you make a profit of £10 on your 1000 shares. The following calculations may make this clearer.

*Outgoings*

| | |
|---|---|
| Buy 1000 GEC call options at 17p. Cost | = £170 |
| Dealing costs | = £35 |
| Exercise option, buy 1000 GEC at 182p. Cost | = £1820 |
| Total buying costs | = £2025 |

The break-even price for the GEC option is 202½p a share

*Income*

| | |
|---|---|
| Sell 1000 GEC at 203½p | = £2035 |
| The 1p rise in GEC share price | = £10 = profit |

At any time during those three months, you can exercise your option to buy 1,000 GEC, then sell them in the market and take your profit. Most option players have no intention of using options to take up stock.

You do not have to take your profit. You can exercise your option after three months, pay the full price for the shares and hold on to them. It is tempting to do this when you have an option which is not going your way. Resist it. Take the loss, and write it off. Do not commit more money to a losing trade.

*Put options*

Put options are like calls, but geared to a fall in the share price. You may think that, say, GEC will drop significantly below the 179p-to-182p market quote over the next three months. A put option costing 17p will buy the right to sell GEC during the next three months at the striking price. The striking price will be at or near the market bid price of 179p. Total cost of 1000 put options will be £204, including commission. So you need GEC to fall by just under 20½p before you break even. For every 1p fall thereafter, you make £10 profit.

So if GEC fall to 145p middle price, and you are able to buy 1000 at 146p, you will have a profit of £126. (That is 179p minus 146p equals 33p, multiplied by 1000, which equals £330. Take away the option cost of £204, including expenses, to leave a profit of £126.)

*Outgoings*

| | |
|---|---|
| Buy 1000 GEC put options at 17p. Cost | = £170 |
| Dealing costs | = £34 |
| Buy 1000 GEC shares at 146p. Cost | = £1460 |
| Total costs | = £1664 |

*Income*

| | |
|---|---|
| Exercise of option to sell 1000 GEC at 179p | = £1790 |
| Profit | = £126 |

Clinch that profit by asking your broker to buy 1000 GEC at 146p. He then exercises your option to 'put' 1000 shares on the option dealer (making him buy them) at the striking price of 179p.

The whole exercise is really like buying a share, and selling it later at a profit. All you have done is reversed the order, buying at a low price and selling at a higher price you fixed earlier with the option.

In the GEC example, only £204 was at risk, and yielded profits of £126, a high percentage return inside three months. In reality, however, GEC is usually too stolid a share to allow such fun, but high returns can be made by using options carefully. The biggest winners are in the most volatile shares.

## Double options

Double options cost nearly twice as much as put or call options, and give the right to buy or sell a share at the striking price over a three-month period. They are expensive, and rarely worth considering.

## Protecting profits with options

Put and call options are not just for gambling in shares that you cannot afford. They can also be used to protect profits. If you fear the market may tumble, but cannot bear to part with some super growth stock, you can have your cake and eat it with options – at a price. Sell the shares and buy a call option in them. That way you unlock your capital and can pop it into some interest-bearing account to sit out the storm. Get it wrong, and your favourite share goes on rising, and you use your call option to buy in again at the pre-determined striking price. If the market does tumble, all you have lost is your option money – and you have been earning interest on your capital to help offset the cost.

Stand the exercise on its head, and you can use put options to protect a profit, too. If you fear a flop-out, keep the shares, but buy

110

put options. If the fall comes, you will make money on the puts to compensate for what you have lost on the shares. Of course, this exercise only makes sense if the shares go back up again later.

These option insurance policies are for the faint-hearted investor. Anyone who paid attention to the earlier passages in this book about buying and selling will have little truck with them. If you feel a fall is coming, sell and try to buy back more cheaply later. Have the courage of your convictions.

### Taking option money

Similar considerations apply, less forcefully, to the business of taking option money. If this sounds too confusing, skip it. Never get into anything you do not understand. But for every option someone buys, someone is selling the option in the hope of profit.

If you buy a call option, someone takes that call money in return for agreeing for three months to sell shares to meet that call. Because there is a jobber in the middle, claiming his piece of the action, the taker of option money does not get the full amount the option buyer pays. So while it might cost 17p to buy a call option in GEC, someone taking that call option might get 12p for agreeing to sell GEC.

For the taker of option money, it means the chance of selling GEC at the striking price, plus a bonus of 12p a share. If GEC do not go up sufficiently for the option to be exercised, the taker gets that 12p without having to sell.

All sorts of plays can be constructed around this: it may be possible to take call money, put money or double option money, or to give put money and take call money at the same time, and so on.

Conventional options can be used in sophisticated combinations, but require careful understanding and a quick eye for an opportunity. If you want to try it, be sure your broker is attuned to what you want to do. It is essential to have a good broker. Be guided by him or her. It is not always possible to take option money – it is only on offer when someone wants to buy an option – so you need someone close to the market.

# TRADED OPTIONS – THE HOTTEST GAME IN TOWN

Traded options have become the hottest game in town since the London Traded Options Market opened on the Stock Exchange floor in 1978. Like conventional options, they offer the right to buy (call) or sell (put) a share at a set price over a pre-determined period.

111

Thereafter, the differences loom large. Traded options are not created by the individual investor, and cannot be taken out in just any share. They are pre-packaged, their form determined by the Options Market. They cover a limited range of shares (but more are being added) and run for three, six or nine months. Call and put contracts are available in a series of pre-determined prices around the current share price. As shares move out of the range of pre-set option prices, new price points are created.

Most important of all, the options themselves can be bought and sold, over and again, until the end of their allotted life. They are traded in contracts that normally represent 1000 shares, so on most contracts a move of 1p in the option value represents a gain or loss of £10.

Confused? You should be. It has taken market hot-shots years to get accustomed to traded options. Even now, many brokers shy away from them. Get them right, though, and there are fat profits to be made – fast. And, unlike conventional options, you can get it wrong in traded options and still sell before you have lost all your money.

### A simple traded option

Try a simple example. Shares in BP, the oil giant, were changing hands at 536p late in April 1986. There were traded option contracts (puts and calls) in BP at 500p, 550p and 600p, each series maturing either in July or October 1986 or in January 1987.

Take the 500p series. A July call cost 55p, an October call 65p, and a January call 83p. On a simple basis, anyone buying the 500p calls in April was hoping for BP shares to be more than 555p in July, 565p in October or 583p in January, against the April market price of 536p.

At 536p, there was already an apparent guaranteed gain on the 500p options. Anyone could have bought, exercised them, and got BP shares at 500p to sell at 536p – a profit of 36p. It would have been daft, of course because the option itself cost 55p, so there would have been a real loss of 19p.

It makes more sense to treat the 19p as the real cost of the option. That is what you would lose by holding the option until it expired in July, assuming BP shares were still 536p then. If BP shares were 560p in July, there would have been a 5p profit (disregarding dealing costs) over the all-in buying price of 555p (500p plus 55p for the option). Pretty dull stuff.

The profit potential should have been better than that, however. Traded option prices are made up of two elements – the intrinsic value, which is related to the underlying share price, and the time

112

value. The time value runs down as an option approaches the end of its life. An option with four weeks to run is worth more than one with only one week to go. So, in the BP example, there is no time value left as the option expires. The option price then is determined solely by the share price.

It is unlikely, however, that BP shares would have risen from 536p to 560p on the last day of the option. Assume that they rose to 545p at the end of April. At that point, the July option would have lost little time value, and the price should have moved up to reflect the increase in BP shares. A 9p gain from 536p to 545p is unlikely to have added 9p to the value of the option, but it could have added 6p, to increase the option to 61p. The potential profit at that stage would be greater than at the end of the life of the option in July when BP shares were actually higher, at 560p.

That is a simple example. The reality is much trickier. The professionals use highly sophisticated formulae to calculate the balance between intrinsic and time values. They can say whether options look dear – or cheap – on their mathematical tables, and deal accordingly. Ask your broker about this before dealing.

### Strips and the naked writer

Straddles, spreads, strips – there are all sorts of manoeuvres that combine different options to achieve various degrees of exposure to risk. Full-time players live in a world of their own, taking advantage of minute-by-minute price fluctuations to turn a penny.

Just as with conventional options, traded options can be used to protect positions in shares you hold. And there are opportunities for taking option money by writing options. You can link this to shares you own, or, more dangerously, to shares you do not own – joining the legendary 'naked writers'. Naked writers sometimes get flogged.

Naked writers apart, traded options hold out the chance of big profits from small share price moves while risking only modest amounts of money. However, the market can be wild and woolly, and it is easy to get wiped out. As ever, you need a clued-up, sympathetic broker. Investors of a nervous disposition should keep well clear of traded options.

If you want to play, the Stock Exchange, very sensibly, requires you first to sign a form signifying that you understand what you are getting into. Before you do, you must read the excellent booklets on traded options prepared by the Stock Exchange. They are invaluable.

## PLAYING FOOTSIE

No matter how terrifying the idea of traded options, everyone should know about Footsie options, which offer the ideal insurance against a market boom or a slump. 'Footsie' is actually the *'Financial Times Stock Exchange 100-Share Index'*. This tracks the prices of 100 of the most highly valued shares to form an index showing which way the market is going.

There is a traded option contract in the Footsie Index, with each point on the index representing a notional £10. Buy Footsie calls if you think the market is going up, or buy Footsie puts if you think it is going down. It is far cheaper than selling all your shares in a panic. Or perhaps you would prefer to sell your shares, put the cash on deposit and buy a Footsie call just in case. Footsie options are a valuable flexible friend in times of uncertainty – or simply an additional gambling counter.

## MARKET GAMBLING WITH A BOOKIE

It is possible to gamble on the market with a bookmaker. The IG Index, Ladbrokes and the City Index take bets on market moves. Their indices do not necessarily coincide with the Stock Exchange figures, but dealing costs can be less than stock market commissions – and profits are free of tax. Stock Exchange traded option profits are caught in the capital gains tax net.

## TAX

Tax? Do not worry about it. Concentrate on making the gains. The first £6300 of realized gains in the tax year 1986-87 is free of capital gains tax. Above that, CGT is charged at 30 per cent.

It is hardly a killer. Add the opportunity of putting £2400 a year (from January 1987) into the Personal Equity Plan, and tax is even less fearsome. You need to do very well on quite a large chunk of cash to make £6300 gains in a year. And you will have more than £6300 of exempt gains when the figure is raised in the 1987 Budget.

## BED AND BREAKFAST

If you are doing well, however, it may make sense to 'bed and breakfast' some profits, or losses. Your broker will give you details.

114

Basically, it involves selling shares (usually near 5 April – the end of the tax year), and buying them back at about the same price a little later. That way, you establish a taxable gain or loss. If you have not used up your full capital gains tax exemption towards the end of one tax year, you can bed and breakfast to crystallize it, and establish a higher starting price in the shares for future CGT purposes. Some licensed dealers offer cheap bed and breakfast services. They might work, but the Inland Revenue might challenge their validity. Be careful.

# 14   Perks – and How to Get Them

Everyone loves something for nothing. No matter how trivial the gifts, shareholders flock to annual meetings of companies where something is given away. And they love the shares which provide the perks, almost regardless of investment merit.

European Ferries, the Townsend Thoresen group, hit a storm when they tried to trim shareholder rights to cut-price trips across the Channel. Eventually the board won, confining the perks to a special class of share, but not before the battle got nasty.

The annual meeting of food group Fitch Lovell used to fill the biggest hall of London's Connaught Rooms, but the meeting itself scarcely mattered. Jovial chairman Sir Ambrose Keevil would dispense good cheer, knowing what everyone was waiting for. The jostling at the end, as shareholders shoved their way out of the hall clutching plastic bags full of loaves, pies, jam and – in the earlier days – a frozen chicken, was an unedifying tribute to shareholder democracy. Sir Ambrose is long gone, and Fitch Lovell no longer give such goodies away.

Go, though, to the meeting of a mighty company such as Grand Metropolitan, and you will hear more questions about cut-price offers of wine, vouchers for Berni Inn steak meals and cheap Camelot holiday week-ends than about profits or dividend prospects.

Serious investors – and if you have ploughed this far, you rank as a serious investor – understand that perks do not matter. Share performance is what counts. Investment value ranks first, second and third. If there are perks, good luck. They should not influence dealing decisions.

If you want them, though, they are all around, involving all sorts of goodies.

*Wimbledon*   Nobody buys All England Lawn Tennis Club Debentures for anything but the perks. Every £50 nominal Debenture carries the right to one free Wimbledon centre court ticket for each day of the Championship in the 1986-90 series, plus entry to the centre court lounge and buffet bar and low-cost reserved parking space adjacent to the centre court. They also carry priority rights for the 1991–5 series. The minimum purchase is two Debentures, which could set you back more than £8000, if you can get them. They do change hands from time to time.

There are other perks which can be quite valuable, if you want to use them, but check first how many shares you need to buy, and how long you need to hold them to qualify.

*Houses*   Buy 1000 shares in Barratt Developments, hold them for at least 12 months, and you can have £500 deducted from the price of a Barratt house for every £25,000 or part of £25,000 you spend. Similar qualifications will result in a discount of between £500 and £2500 on a Bellway house.

*Cars*   Several garage groups give discounts on new cars. They include Alexanders Holdings, Barr & Wallace Arnold, Henlys, Lonrho (sometimes) and Manor National.

*Cruises*   A mere 250 shares in Trafalgar House entitles you to a 10 per cent discount on most QE2 and Sagafjord world cruises, plus a 15 per cent discount on other cruises and at Cunard hotels in the UK and the Caribbean.

*Holidays and hotels*   A 10 per cent discount on their package holidays comes from Horizon, and from Rank, who own OSL, Wings, Ellerman, Sunflight and Freshfields Holidays. Both have a limit of up to £1000 holiday value. LWT offer 10 per cent off their holiday operations, and numerous brewers and hotel groups have cheap weekends to shareholders.

*Food*   Kennedy Brookes, who own many of the middle-range restaurants in London, give a 20 per cent discount to holders of 500 shares. Assorted brewers and hotel groups also offer cheap meals.

*Drink*   Several brewers and hotel groups feature special offers to shareholders, or supply free drinks at the annual meeting.

*Clothes*   Burton Group give some vouchers allowing a 20 per cent discount; Next allow 25 per cent off any one purchase; Cecil Gee give vouchers; and Moss Bros take 10 per cent off almost everything for those holding 250 shares for six months. Austin Reed give a 15 per cent discount and menswear group John Kent knock 10 per cent off, both for holders of 500 shares. At the top end, Gieves Group give anyone holding 600 shares for three months a reduction of 20 per cent at branches of Gieves & Hawkes.

*Cleaning*  Sketchley send a 25 per cent discount card if you have 300 shares.

*Jewellery*  Aspreys offer a 15 per cent discount card when holders of 375 shares are registered.

*Electrical goods*  Emess Lighting knock 25 per cent off a range of light fittings if you have 100 shares. Ladbroke offer 7·5 per cent off at their Laskys electrical shops.

*Do-it-yourself*  Lots of offers here, including up to 25 per cent off items at Manders Holdings, 12·5 per cent off Weatherseal double glazing and such from London & Northern, 10 per cent off Banbury windows, etc. from London & Midland, a 10 per cent reduction at Leyland Paint & Wallpaper shops, and 15 per cent off Sharps' fitted bedrooms from Hawley Group.

There are more, many more perks, and the list is growing all of the time. At annual meetings, reluctant company chairmen frequently find themselves badgered to make special offers. Be careful, though, for the list changes frequently. Offers are withdrawn from time to time, companies get taken over and – take special note – several that were fond of giving freebies have disappeared or hit hard times.

Some brokers compile lists of shareholder perks. Best known are Seymour Pierce & Co., 10 Old Jewry, London EC2R 8EA, who make a small charge for their list. Brokers Kleinwort Grieveson, 20 Fenchurch Street, London EC3P 3DB, also supply a perks list.

# 15　A Final Warning

It will take a while before the fall-out from the Big Bang settles and everyone has a clear idea of the new way of the investment world. A few words of warning might, however, be helpful.

Perfectly respectable people might ring to try to sell you shares. Absolutely crooked ones might ring too. No matter what they say, never buy from strangers over the telephone. Never commit yourself. Ask them to put their ideas in writing, then check them with your broker, banker or someone else. You could also try the *Daily Mail* City page, perhaps – but in writing, please.

They may say you will miss the chance of a lifetime by delaying a day or two. Never mind. Play safe. The villains trade on greed and gullibility. They are doing you a favour, they say, by calling. They want to impress you, and make sure their first trade with you is a winner, so you will trade again. Do not listen.

*Never, never, never* buy from the man from Madrid. Or Brussels. Or some other foreign shore. And be careful about eager salespeople from Britain.

*Never, never, never* be tempted into gambling in commodities, futures or options, other than through a stockbroker you know and trust. The person who telephones you with a deal – any deal – always has an angle: he wants your money.

If you think trading shares on the London Stock Exchange is tricky and dangerous, you ain't seen nothing yet. For all of its faults, our stock market plays reasonably fair, and most of the people there are honourable. Stick to it. Do not be sucked into more exotic markets. Learning about the Stock Exchange can take a lifetime. Leave the rest to others.

Good luck.

# Useful Addresses

## THE STOCK EXCHANGE

*London*: London EC2N 1HP, tel: (01) 588 2355.

*Belfast*: Northern Bank House, 10 High Street, Belfast BT1 2BP, tel: (0232) 221094.

*Birmingham*: Margaret Street, Birmingham B3 3JL, tel: (021) 236 9181.

*Bristol*: St Nicholas Street, Bristol BS1 1TH, tel: (0272) 24541.

*Dublin*: 28 Anglesea Street, Dublin 2, tel: (0001) 778808.

*Glasgow*: 69 St George's Place, Glasgow G2 1BU, tel: (041) 221 7060.

*Liverpool*: Silkhouse Court, Tithebarn Street, Liverpool L2 2LT, tel: (051) 236 0869.

*Manchester*: 6 Norfolk Street, Manchester M2 1DS, tel: (061) 833 0931.

## INVESTMENT TRUSTS

Foreign & Colonial Investment Trust, 1 Laurence Pountney Hill, London EC4R 0BA.

Globe Investment Trust, Electra House, Temple Place, Victoria Embankment, London WC2R 3HP.

Scottish American Investment Trust, 45 Charlotte Square, Edinburgh EH2 4HW.

# Index

Account trading, 29-30
  end-account selling, 98-9
Acorn computers, 45
'Actuaries' Share Indices, *Financial Times*, 48
Albert Fisher company, 83
Alexanders Holdings, 117
Alexanders, Laing & Cruickshank, stockbrokers, 51, 60
Allders department stores, 14
Amstrad word processors, 83
Annual meetings, 12, 82
Arbib, Martyn, 3
Aspreys, 118
Asset backing, 49-50
Auditors' reports, 17-18
Austin Reed, 177
Averaging, 94

Balance sheets, 16-17
Banbury windows, 118
Banks, use of, 25
Barclays Bank, 59
Barclays Merchant Bank, 40, 78
Barings, 40, 78
Barr & Wallace Arnold, 117
Barratt Developments, 117
Beckman, Bob, newsletters, 55-6
Bed and breakfasting profits and losses, 114-15
Bid stocks, suitable, 72-5; capital returns, 73; leaks of intentions, 74, 75; profit margins, 73; share stakes in target company, 74; tired

families, 73
  *See also* Takeover bids
Big Bang the, xi, 22-4, 27, 28, 30, 40, 85
Blue chips, 59-60
Boardroom bust-ups, 97-8
BOC, xii, 4
Boesky, Ivan, 76
Bookmakers and gambling on the market, 114
Boots, 59
Borrie, Sir Gordon, 22
BP, 112-13
B.R.I. Information Services Ltd, 90
British Gas, xi, 9
British Home Stores, 72, 80
British Telecom, xi, 9, 37, 41
Brown Shipley, 40
Building societies, 2, 32
Burberrys, 14
Burton Group, 4, 73, 80, 117
Business cycles, 99

Capital gains tax, 114
Capital growth or income, 5-6
Cazenove, stockbrokers, 40
Cecil Gee company, 117
Chairmen's statements, 14, 84-5
Charterhouse investment bank, 40, 78
Charts, 88-91; activities of chartists, 88-9; bar, 88; figure, 88; and insider dealing, 90; point, 88; value of, 89-90

121